NEW THINKING & OLD REALITIES

THE JOHNS HOPKINS
FOREIGN POLICY INSTITUTE

The Johns Hopkins Foreign Policy Institute (FPI) was established in 1980 as an integral part of the Paul H. Nitze School of Advanced International Studies (SAIS) in Washington, D.C., to unite the worlds of scholarship and public affairs in the search for realistic answers to contemporary problems facing the United States. The FPI is a meeting place for SAIS faculty members and students as well as for government analysts, policymakers, diplomats, journalists, business leaders, and other specialists in international affairs.

Research activities at the FPI span the spectrum of U.S. foreign policy and international affairs. Current FPI programs examine the future of U.S.-Soviet relations; evolving roles in the Atlantic Alliance; the relation of arms control to force structure and military-political doctrine; the political implications of the U.S.-Canada free trade agreement; the role of the media in foreign policy; comparative U.S. and Soviet national security policy making; patterns of Third World conflict; processes of multilateral negotiations; the global environment and resource depletion; and other leading international concerns.

In addition to books and monographs on a broad range of foreign and defense policy issues, FPI publications include: the *SAIS Review*, a semiannual journal of international affairs that is edited by SAIS students; the FPI Policy Briefs, a series of analyses of immediate or emerging foreign policy issues; the FPI Case Studies, a series designed to teach analytical negotiating skills; the FPI Consensus Reports, which present recommendations on a series of critical foreign policy issues; and the Energy Papers, presenting new research on international energy resource issues.

For additional information, write to: Director of Publications, The Paul H. Nitze School of Advanced International Studies, The Johns Hopkins Foreign Policy Institute, 1619 Massachusetts Avenue, N.W., Washington, D.C. 20036-2297.

NEW THINKING

& OLD REALITIES

America, Europe, and Russia

Michael T. Clark and Simon Serfaty,

Editors

Published in association with
The Johns Hopkins Foreign Policy Institute

SEVEN LOCKS PRESS
WASHINGTON

Library of Congress Cataloging-in-Publication Data

New thinking & old realities: America, Europe, and Soviet Russia /
    Michael T. Clark and Simon Serfaty, editors.
        p.   cm.
    "Published in association with the Johns Hopkins Foreign Policy
Institute."
    Includes bibliographical references and index.
    ISBN 0-932020-90-9 (cloth): $24.95. — ISBN 0-932020-89-5 (paper) :
$13.95
    1. World politics—1985-1995.   2. Europe—Politics and
government—1945- . I. Clark, Michael T. (Michael Thomas), 1957-
II. Serfaty, Simon. III. Johns Hopkins Unviersity. Foreign Policy Institute.
IV. Title: New thinking and old realities.
D849.N5 1991
909.82'8—dc20   90-8999
                                                            CIP

Typesetting by Steve Brigham
Cover design by New Age Graphics, Bethesda, MD
Printed by McNaughton and Gunn, Saline, MI

Printed on acid-free paper

Manufactured in the United States of America

For more information, write or call:

Seven Locks Press
P.O. Box 27
Cabin John, MD 20818
(301) 320-2130

Contents

Editors and Contributors

Michael T. Clark is assistant professor of international politics and political theory at the College of William & Mary. The managing editor of The Johns Hopkins Foreign Policy Institute (FPI) publications from 1988 to 1990, he is the author of various publications on U.S. relations with Latin America.

Simon Serfaty is executive director of the FPI and research professor of American foreign policy at the Paul H. Nitze School of Advanced International Studies (SAIS). He is the author of *American Foreign Policy in a Hostile World: Dangerous Years* (1984) and *After Reagan: False Starts, Missed Opportunities and New Beginnings* (1989), among numerous other works.

Anne Henderson is assistant professor of government at the College of William & Mary. Her work includes articles on East European relations with the International Monetary Fund and on the politics of Western investment in Eastern Europe.

Josef Joffe is foreign editor and columnist for the *Süddeutsche Zeitung* in Munich and the Beton Michael Kaneb Professor of National Security Affairs at Harvard (1990–1991). He is the author of *The Troubled Partnership: Europe, the U.S. and the Burdens of Alliance* (1987).

George Liska is Paul H. Nitze Professor of international politics at SAIS. His latest book is *The Ways of Power: Pattern and Meaning in World Politics* (1990).

Ilya Prizel is associate professor and acting director of Soviet studies at SAIS. He is the author of *Latin America Through Soviet Eyes* (1990) and is currently writing a book on Soviet relations with Poland and Germany.

John Van Oudenaren is associate head of the department of political science at the RAND Corporation. He is the author of *Détente in Europe: The Soviet Union and the West Since 1953* (1991).

Preface

T HAT THE INTERNATIONAL SYSTEM is now undergoing a transformation is well understood by many. How far the potential of these changes reaches is less obvious, and, apart from a broad faith that they are bound to be salutary in their impact, what implications these events might have for America's role and purpose in the world is understood, even by experts, barely at all. There is clearly a need, therefore, for viewing the momentous events of 1989 in some broader perspective and for taking our bearings from some deeper historical patterns and trends. Hence, this collection of essays.

As the title of this volume suggests, the contributors take as their starting point the confrontation between the "new thinking" of Soviet President Mikhail Gorbachev and of his visionary counterparts in Europe and America and the "old realities" of international statecraft. The impact of new thinking is gauged by measuring the changes taking place in a number of distinct, but overlapping and interrelated spheres, against old realities that are defined by reference to a historical framework encompassing, at a minimum, the entire post–World War II era or, on the outside, the life of the Peace-of-Westphalia international system. Only by setting the events of the past year and those currently taking place in such a context is it possible even to begin to weigh their implications for the future or devise a strategy to shape it.

The essays in this volume have been arranged to reflect its thematic counterpoint. Thus, the first three chapters seek to explain the origins, aims, and significance of the radical turnabout in Soviet policy toward Western Europe (John Van Oudenaren), Eastern Europe (Anne Henderson), and the world beyond (Ilya Prizel) that has taken place during the past year. Seen in its totality, this event augurs the end not only of the Cold War, but of the international order to which it gave rise.

The second set of essays is concerned with the persistent influence of realities older than the Cold War—in concrete terms, with the always unsettling fact of German national cohesion and material strength; more broadly, with the possibilities of transcending the traditional methods of statecraft and their unhappy consequences. The first study of the second series (Josef Joffe) thus analyzes the present manifestation of modern Europe's most ancient dilemma: how to balance the legitimate claims of German nationhood against the equally legitimate claims of European security. The second essay (Simon Serfaty) analyzes the approach to this problem evolved during the Cold War in Europe's western half, with the ambivalent support of the United States; the third (George Liska) examines an alternative in keeping with the more distant history and culture of Europe's eastern half, including the European parts of Soviet Russia.

The volume concludes with a review essay (Michael Clark) that seeks to highlight and connect recurrent themes in all six studies as a way of approaching the question: What is living and what is dead in the philosophy—realism—that has guided the practice of American and Western foreign policy through the Cold War?

Despite the richness and subtlety of the themes treated here, every effort has been made to present these essays in a manner that is broadly accessible. In each case, the authors have endeavored to provide an analysis of recent events that may prove as illuminating to the public at large as they should be to statesmen and other professional students of contemporary history. The spirit of these essays is therefore in keeping with the essential mandate of The Johns Hopkins Foreign Policy Institute (FPI) of the Paul H. Nitze School of Advanced International Studies (SAIS): to make available to the policy community and the interested public the most useful in contemporary scholarship.

Michael T. Clark and Simon Serfaty

August 1990

PART ONE

New Thinking:
The Revolutions of 1989

I

Gorbachev and His Predecessors: Two Faces of New Thinking

John Van Oudenaren

I N POLICY TOWARD WESTERN EUROPE, Mikhail Gorbachev initially played a weak domestic and foreign policy hand with remarkable skill and a fair amount of luck. He managed to put the conservative governments of Western Europe and the United States on the defensive and to attenuate the "enemy image" of the Soviet Union that for four decades was responsible for NATO's cohesiveness. The highpoint of Gorbachev's success came in the late spring and early summer of 1989, when he made his triumphant visit to West Germany and outlined his vision of a common European home in a speech to the Parliamentary Assembly of the Council of Europe in Strasbourg.

Yet in the second half of 1989, Gorbachev's luck ran out, as his political and public relations skills proved irrelevant to a series of developments that called into question the very basis of Soviet power in Europe. Beginning with the formation of a non-Communist government in Poland in August and ending with the violent upheavals in Romania in December, the East European countries in varying degrees all turned toward political pluralism and market economic systems. By the end of the year, the two Soviet-led multilateral organizations in Europe—the Warsaw Treaty Organization (WTO) and the Council for Mutual Economic Assistance (CMEA)—were in total disarray. In early 1990 the Soviet Union agreed to withdraw its troops from Hungary and

This essay, now much revised, was originally prepared and presented as part of a series of lectures organized by the Department of European Studies at the School of Advanced International Studies with the support of the German Marshall Fund of the United States.

Czechoslovakia and to begin negotiations that were expected to formalize the unification of Germany and the liquidation of a separate German socialist state.

This chapter examines the Gorbachev record in policy toward Western Europe. Beginning with a discussion of his inheritance from the "era of stagnation," it analyzes the successes of his policy from 1986 to early 1989 and looks at the challenges posed by the subsequent changes in Eastern Europe.

II

The hand that Gorbachev inherited in 1985 was weak in three respects. First, his own personal power was limited. Although the details of the Kremlin succession process are largely unknown to outsiders, evidence suggests that Gorbachev was chosen largely because there was no obvious alternative. He did not assume office with a broad mandate to make radical departures in foreign and domestic policy.

Second, the Soviet internal economic and social situation was bad and looked increasingly worse to Gorbachev and his advisers as they began examining problems and attempting solutions. Gorbachev started out as a fairly conventional leader, stressing the need for "acceleration" *(uskorenie)*, which was to be accomplished by greater discipline, improved leadership, and selective reform and "restructuring" *(perestroika)*. But by the summer of 1986, Gorbachev's thinking had undergone a marked radicalization. He began to downplay "acceleration" as a short-term goal and instead to stress a more fundamental, comprehensive and possibly decades-long process of "restructuring" in all areas of national life: economic, social, cultural, political, and psychological. *Glasnost* (openness) and democratization emerged as important instruments of the restructuring campaign.

Third, and most important for understanding Gorbachev's actions, the international situation facing the USSR in early 1985 was difficult, although somewhat improved from the low point of late 1983 and early 1984. The early 1980s had been a period of foreign policy setbacks for the Soviet Union, not only in Europe, but in other parts of the world as well. Despite appeals to West European leaders and a massive peace campaign directed at the opposition political parties and the public at large, the Soviet Union had failed to derail NATO's 1979 "two-track" decision to deploy new U.S. intermediate-range nuclear forces (INF) in Europe in response to the earlier Soviet deployment of modernized SS-20 missiles. The Soviets compounded their INF difficulties in December 1983 by walking out of the nuclear arms control talks to protest the first deployments. Hoping by their action to trigger a crisis in the Western alliance, they instead found themselves isolated.

Another major European foreign policy problem arose out of the crisis in Poland, which erupted in August 1980 with the birth of *Solidarity* and was brought under control but by no means solved by the imposition of martial law in December 1981. The Polish crisis led to heightened recriminations between the Soviet and West European governments and very nearly caused the breakdown of the follow-up meeting of the Conference on Security and Cooperation in Europe (CSCE). More important, it called into question a fundamental premise of the Brezhnev détente policy as it had developed after the 1968 invasion of Czechoslovakia: that a stable Eastern Europe made possible a more active Soviet policy toward Western Europe, which in turn would help to further stabilize Eastern Europe by providing concrete benefits (such as expanded trade and credit flows) and eliminating the Western Cold War challenge to the legitimacy and permanence of "socialist achievements" east of the Elbe.

In addition to the INF and Polish challenges, the Soviet leaders faced a range of other foreign policy problems: the war in Afghanistan, the U.S. defense buildup (and especially the Strategic Defense Initiative), continuing differences with Japan over the Northern Territories and with China over Afghanistan, Vietnam, and Soviet force levels in Asia, and the growing irrelevance of the Soviet Union to the concerns of major Third World countries such as Brazil, Mexico, and Indonesia. Most of these problems were not directly related to the situation in Europe, but they contributed to a general impression that Soviet policy had lost momentum and lacked imagination.

These foreign policy problems were of course counterbalanced somewhat by the difficulties confronting Western governments. The Soviet Union lost the INF struggle, but the West's victory was costly, as the defense consensus in Western Europe was shattered when the West German Social Democratic Party (SPD), British Labour, and the "Scandilux" parties veered sharply to the left. The conservative and centrist political parties that had carried out the INF deployments emerged from the struggle politically and psychologically battered and determined not to go through a similar episode. In West Germany, Foreign Minister and Free Democratic Party (FPD) leader Hans Dietrich Genscher had risked the very survival of his party in breaking with the SPD, largely over the INF issue; the majority Christian Democratic Union/Christian Social Union (CDU/CSU) was less scarred by the INF struggle, but by no means eager to repeat the experience.

The internal crises in Poland and Afghanistan created enormous problems for the Soviet leadership, but they also led to increased tensions in U.S.-West European relations, as the Carter and Reagan administrations demanded and the West Europeans generally resisted economic and other sanctions. These tensions reached their peak in mid-1982 with the gas pipeline dispute between the United States and the four largest members of the European Community (EC). The United States resolutely opposed, but ultimately failed to prevent, the extension of large financial credits by the West European governments to fund construction of the pipeline. SDI presented a long-term challenge to Soviet power, but it also proved useful as an issue around which to mobilize West European opinion against the United States, to deflect attention from the Soviet defeat on INF, and to inflame the already sensitive issues of technology transfer and European "self-assertion."

From Gorbachev's point of view, it also was fortunate that the Chernenko regime, for all its perceived weakness, had managed to bring some of the most acute foreign policy problems under control, thus sparing the new leader the need to make difficult decisions and highly visible concessions. Foreign Minister Andrei Gromyko had gotten the U.S.-Soviet arms control talks back on track in his meetings with President Ronald Reagan in September 1984 and with Secretary of State George Shultz in January 1985. Poland and the Soviet Union concluded a major trade and economic integration agreement in early 1984, and the Soviets had contributed to what they hoped was a process of stabilization and "normalization" in Poland by supporting the government of Gen. Wojciech Jaruzelski. Going further back, Brezhnev had begun a modest rapprochement with China in 1982 and had undertaken two quasi-doctrinal revisions that paved the way to Gorbachev's "new political thinking": In 1977, he introduced the "Tula line," which eschewed military superiority, and in 1982, he issued a unilateral declaration pledging that the Soviet Union would never be the first to use nuclear weapons in the event of war.

There is little evidence that Gorbachev took power having fundamentally rethought Soviet objectives in Europe. Precisely what those objectives were of course had become a standing controversy in the West as early as the 1950s. Some observers claimed that the Soviet Union sought to eliminate the American military and political presence from Europe, while others argued that the Soviet leadership actually favored an American presence as a stabilizing influence and a check on a potentially resurgent West Germany.

One of the most telling pieces of evidence in this controversy came from Gorbachev's own foreign minister Eduard Shevardnadze, who told an interviewer in early 1990 that until "quite recently our aim was to oust the Americans from Europe at any price."[1] In particular, the centerpiece of this long-standing Soviet campaign to "oust" the Americans had always been a vociferous opposition to the deployment of U.S.

---

1. *Izvestiia*, February 20, 1990.

nuclear weapons on the continent. This opposition reflects a keen awareness of the political as much as the strategic importance of these weapons. They have been the glue that held the NATO alliance together, as well as the weapons that posed the greatest direct threat to Soviet security. But their sheer destructiveness and the fact that they were controlled by a transoceanic government made them unpopular with some elites and large segments of the population. They thus became a logical focus of Soviet propaganda and arms control efforts. As will be seen, Gorbachev was, if anything, more active than his predecessors in promoting the denuclearization of Europe.

In one respect, however, Shevardnadze's admission that a Soviet objective was to oust the Americans from Europe at any price was an evident exaggeration. The price that all Soviet leaders since Stalin had shown they were not prepared to pay was surrender of the Soviet sphere of influence in Eastern Europe and East Germany. When Gorbachev came to power, the Soviet Union had not made a credible German reunification offer since the early 1950s. And its interventions in Czechoslovakia in 1968 and (indirectly) in Poland in 1980-1981 had helped to keep alive a sense of the Soviet threat in Europe that in turn generated political support for the American presence. A second and even more important Soviet objective thus was to maintain control of Eastern Europe.

A third traditional objective of Soviet policy was to forestall progress toward a united Western Europe. In the Soviet view, such a "Europe" would constitute a potential security threat to the Soviet Union, be subject to West German domination, and represent a magnet for Eastern Europe. This wariness of West European unification in part accounted for the Soviet Union's long-standing refusal to recognize the Community.

IV

During his initial year in power, Gorbachev showed little interest in departing from these touchstones of Soviet strategic thinking, but proceeded along fairly traditional lines in his policy toward Western Europe, working through long-established mechanisms and institutions, albeit with greater energy and more tactical flexibility than his predecessors had shown. In May 1985, he reactivated efforts, which the USSR had been making off and on since 1976, to reach some kind of umbrella agreement between the European Community and the Council for Mutual Economic Assistance. In a shift in Soviet attitudes toward the Community, he appeared to recognize its "political" character, telling Italian Prime Minister Bettino Craxi that "insofar as the EEC countries act as a 'political entity,' we are prepared to seek a common language on concrete international problems with it."[2] Gorbachev's recognition of the EC was cautious and qualified, however, and marked a logical continuation of a trend that had begun in the early 1970s with Brezhnev's de facto recognition of the Community much more than a bold new departure.

In April 1985, Gorbachev announced a six-month moratorium on the deployment of SS-20s, which again reflected more a shift in tactics than aims. This gesture was directed at public opinion in the Netherlands, the only basing country yet to adopt a final decision on deployment. In mid-1985, the Soviet Union also began negotiating more seriously than hitherto in the Stockholm Conference on Disarmament in Europe (CDE). On balance, however, Gorbachev did not begin to make major innovations in Soviet arms control policy until his second year in power.

Gorbachev's courtship of the European non-Communist Left and in particular the West German SPD was also consistent with earlier policy. Among his first high-level guests in Moscow were SPD Chairman and President of the Socialist International Willy Brandt, Swedish Prime Minister Olof Palme, Craxi, and a delegation from the Socialist International Disarmament Advisory Commission (SIDAC). While stepping up ties with the West German Social Democrats, Gorbachev

---

2. *Pravda*, May 30, 1985.

continued and, in some respects, intensified the freeze in relations with the West German government that had been in effect since late 1983 and the initial INF deployments. At Chernenko's funeral, Chancellor Helmut Kohl was accorded only perfunctory treatment. And throughout the spring of 1985, Soviet pronouncements on Germany remained harsh as the USSR moved toward its triumphant celebration of the fortieth anniversary of victory in Europe.

While maintaining the chill in Soviet-West German relations, Gorbachev visited France in September 1985 and attempted to revive the special relationship that French President François Mitterrand had deliberately downgraded after taking power in 1981. Although the visit was useful in deflating the importance of the U.S.-Soviet summit scheduled for November, it did not fully accomplish its intended results in Europe. The French turned aside offers for separate negotiations on INF and were critical of Gorbachev's handling of human rights and emigration. Mitterrand refused to issue a joint communiqué or to agree to resume the regularized summitry that had been established by Charles de Gaulle and that had flourished under Georges Pompidou and Valéry Giscard d'Estaing.

In hindsight, the most important aspect of Gorbachev's early foreign policy was what he did not do—namely, turn his back on the United States for the duration of the Reagan term. In the early part of Gorbachev's tenure, a number of Western experts purported to see evidence of an emerging "Yakovlev line" in Soviet foreign policy. When fully implemented, this "line" (which took its name from Aleksandr Yakovlev, the former Soviet ambassador to Canada and a close Gorbachev adviser) was expected to entail a relative downgrading of the importance of the United States and a corresponding turn toward the other "centers" of "world imperialism"—Western Europe and Japan. But Gorbachev clearly chose not to follow this course—if indeed it was ever recommended to him.

Gorbachev and Reagan met in Geneva in November 1985 in the first of five such meetings in various cities. After a somewhat rocky start, Eduard Shevardnadze (who had replaced Gromyko in July 1985) proceeded to develop a close personal relationship with Shultz. These meetings ultimately resulted in one important U.S.-Soviet agreement with implications for Europe—the INF treaty of December 1987—and helped to facilitate the agreement leading to the Soviet withdrawal from Afghanistan and the start of new conventional arms control talks in Europe.

V

The initial radicalization of Gorbachev's foreign policy probably grew out of a combination of factors, including disappointment with the Geneva summit, the approach of the 27th Congress of the Communist Party of the Soviet Union (CPSU), and a growing awareness of Soviet economic difficulties. Gorbachev and Reagan both came away from Geneva claiming modest gains. Reagan could point to language in the concluding joint statement that endorsed his goals of deep cuts in strategic forces and an interim INF agreement, while Gorbachev and his advisers expressed satisfaction that they had secured a passage in the joint statement affirming "that a nuclear war cannot be won and must never be fought." Soviet officials invoked this pledge against SDI (with its essentially "war-fighting" rationale) and hinted that it had implications for extended deterrence as well.

In truth, however, Gorbachev had reason to be less than fully satisfied with the Geneva outcome. Despite heated discussions with Reagan, he was unable to make headway against SDI. The joint statement basically sidestepped the issue by repeating the formulation used in a January 1985 Shultz-Gromyko statement. In addition, Gorbachev committed himself to two follow-on summits that he must have known would be politically beneficial to Reagan.

The year after the Geneva summit thus witnessed a series of Soviet moves that appear to have been aimed at seizing the initiative on the nuclear issue and placing the United States on the defensive. Gorbachev had already taken a step in this direction with his unilateral nuclear test moratorium of August 1985, but this had largely fallen flat. On January 15, 1986, some six weeks after the Geneva summit, Gorbachev unveiled a three-stage plan for the total elimination of nuclear weapons by the year 2000. The following month, in his report to the 27th Party Congress, he outlined a plan for the creation of a "comprehensive system of international security."

The January 15 plan was a curious mix of utopian elements and concrete proposals that had several implications for Soviet policy toward Western Europe. It strongly suggested that in negotiating the "interim" INF agreement endorsed in the Geneva statement, the Soviet Union would not agree to reduced but equal levels of Soviet and American INF (that is, the "walk in the woods" agreement U.S. and Soviet negotiators had worked out privately, but that had been rejected by both the Soviet and U.S. governments). The first stage of the plan, which was to last five to eight years, called for the "liquidation" of all U.S. and Soviet INF "in the European zone" and a freeze on French and British nuclear arsenals. The plan also signaled a stepped-up Soviet campaign for the elimination of all nuclear weapons from Europe.

In addition, the new Soviet position indirectly contributed to the adoption of a more active Soviet approach to conventional arms control. When Soviet envoys went to European capitals to brief governments on the plan, they found the reaction largely negative. The West Germans in particular complained that the plan did not address the problem of conventional and chemical imbalances favoring the Soviet Union. Gorbachev's April 18 speech in East Berlin, in which he called for an agreement on "substantial reductions in all the components of the land forces and tactical air forces of the European states and the relevant forces of the USA and Canada deployed in Europe,"[3] appears to have been in part a Soviet response to these complaints. Subsequently, of course,

---

3. *Pravda*, April 19, 1986.

conventional arms reduction developed a momentum of its own, particularly as Soviet economic conditions worsened and as Gorbachev sought to trim military outlays, but his initial Atlantic-to-the-Urals proposal appears to have been linked to the denuclearization goal.

Although the Soviet proposals of early 1986 were appealing to some in Western Europe and the United States, they did not lead to the immediate breakthrough that Gorbachev seemed to desire. In the spring of 1986, U.S.-Soviet diplomacy bogged down as Shevardnadze put off a planned trip to Washington to protest the U.S. bombing of Libya and as Gorbachev himself confronted his first severe crisis—the Chernobyl disaster—the handling of which did little to allay Western suspicion of the "new" Soviet foreign policy. At the same time, Gorbachev started edging away from his commitment to follow-on summits with Reagan. In April, for example, he stated that summits in Washington or Moscow were out of the question, but that he would be willing to meet with Reagan in London to sign a ban on nuclear tests.

In late May, Gorbachev undertook his own high-profile effort to restore momentum to Soviet diplomacy. In an unprecedented gesture for a party general secretary, he went to the foreign ministry to address a closed meeting of officials and ambassadors, many of whom had returned to Moscow especially to attend. According to a brief TASS report, the conference was devoted to the subject of "implementing the decisions of the CPSU Congress in the field of foreign policy."[4] Additional details of the conference were not made public, but it was rumored that its convening reflected Gorbachev's dissatisfaction with the performance of Soviet diplomacy and his concern that foreign audiences were not

---

4. TASS, May 23, 1986; "Diplomats Hear Critical Speech by Gorbachev," *Los Angeles Times*, May 25, 1986; Serge Schemann, "Gorbachev Gives Critique of Soviet Foreign Policy," *New York Times*, May 24, 1986. A detailed summary of the speech was published a year later in *Vestnik MID*, No. 1, 1987. The full text has not been published.

responding favorably enough to his recent initiatives, notably his January 15 plan.

The May 23 speech clearly was a turning point in Soviet diplomacy. It was followed by the tabling, in June 1986, of a more realistic Soviet Strategic Arms Reduction Talks (START) proposal, which in turn led to an active correspondence between Gorbachev and Reagan. Throughout the summer the two men exchanged letters in which each sought to top the other with proposals for extravagant nuclear reductions. This correspondence in turn set the stage for the Reykjavík meeting of October 1986.

Agreeing to meet in Reykjavík was Gorbachev's way of solving the summit dilemma that he had faced since the Geneva meeting late the previous year. Much to the frustration of the American side, he was determined not to give Reagan a high-profile Washington summit, particularly in the absence of some satisfaction on the issues of greatest concern to the Soviet side: SDI and nuclear testing. By proposing the interim summit in Iceland, he appeared to keep his own commitment to follow-on meetings, while avoiding what he feared would be a U.S.-hosted public relations triumph for Reagan.

From the European perspective, the most important result of Reykjavík was the agreement to seek a zero-zero solution on INF. The zero solution initially was part of a package deal trading Soviet acceptance of the destruction of all INF for U.S. concessions on SDI, but it was widely expected that Gorbachev eventually would "delink" the two issues, thereby opening the way to an arms control agreement that would eliminate from the continent Soviet SS-20s, SS-4s, and SS-5s as well as U.S. Pershing II and cruise missiles. Gorbachev finally took this step on February 28, 1987.

Although both sides were now committed to the zero option in principle, important details remained. In working out arrangements to prevent circumvention of the INF agreement at the level of short-range intermediate nuclear forces (SRINF), Gorbachev offered Shultz a "second zero." Shultz then, in effect, presented the Western allies with an ultimatum, insisting that they either accept the Gorbachev offer or agree to a new and, at the time, entirely unfeasible SRINF modernization program. When the alliance accepted, the Soviets upped the ante, insisting that the second zero include the warheads for the 72 German-owned Pershing IA missiles. Chancellor Kohl ultimately yielded on this issue, thereby clearing the way to the conclusion of the INF treaty and its signature at the December 1987 Washington summit.

Whatever the merits and demerits of the double-zero agreement, one side effect was a sense of disappointment in West Germany among those conservative and centrist forces that had strongly supported the United States on defense issues. Some in the CDU/CSU felt that the United States had joined with Gorbachev in imposing his denuclearization agenda on the alliance, in large part for U.S. domestic political reasons. The Left, in contrast, welcomed the new agreement, arguing that it did not represent a vindication of those who had argued the need to deal with the Soviet Union from a position of strength, but rather that it should be seen as the first stage toward further denuclearization through negotiations with a new and enlightened Soviet leadership.

V

Until the end of 1987, the focus of Gorbachev's policy toward Western Europe was to solve the INF problem, which could only be done by dealing with the United States. Thus, although Western Europe was to some extent an object of U.S.-Soviet diplomacy, direct contact with West European leaders was limited. After his October 1985 visit to France, Gorbachev did not travel to Western Europe until April 1989. There were, nonetheless, a number of low-key breakthroughs in Soviet-West European relations at both the bilateral and multilateral levels during this period.

On the bilateral level, Gorbachev showed some preference for dealing with Britain's Prime Minister Margaret Thatcher, who was valued for her perceived influence over President Reagan. There was a slow warming of Franco-Soviet relations, and in July 1986, Mitterrand went to the USSR to watch the launch of a Soviet spacecraft whose crew included a French astronaut. Relations with West Germany remained cool, however. Contrary to what had been predicted by some observers as the INF crisis neared its climax, the Soviet Union did not sever or even drastically curtail economic, cultural, scientific, and other forms of cooperation. But the Soviet leadership did place a de facto ban on high-level travel to Bonn. Genscher's July 1986 visit to Moscow raised expectations in Bonn that this ban was about to be lifted, but relations deteriorated once again in the fall of that year as the result of comments by Chancellor Kohl comparing Gorbachev to Joseph Goebbels, the Nazi propaganda chief. Despite the written apology that Genscher presented to Shevardnadze at the opening of the Vienna CSCE review conference, the Soviets chose not to be mollified.

In mid-1987, the Soviet government began stepping up contacts with virtually every political leader in West Germany but Kohl. In July, President Richard von Weizsäcker went to Moscow for a state visit. Other prominent West German visitors included Bavarian Prime Minister Franz-Josef Strauss in December 1987 and Lothar Späth, the prime minister of Baden-Württemberg in February 1988. Meanwhile, Foreign Minister Genscher made five unreciprocated visits to Moscow (prompting criticism in Germany) before Shevardnadze made a return visit in January 1988. A Kohl visit to Moscow finally took place in October 1988, but the Soviet welcome was restrained (as the *Economist* remarked, "on the whole it was the steely, not the cuddly, Mr. Gorbachev whom Mr. Kohl met") despite the fact that the West Germans brought a large contingent of business executives and concluded a number of deals, including a DM3 billion line of credit.[5]

---

5. *Economist*, October 29, 1988.

VI

In his May 1986 speech to the Ministry of Foreign Affairs, Gorbachev praised the abandonment of what he called "dogmatic" positions with respect to the EC. The pace of negotiations between the EC and CMEA subsequently quickened, leading to the initialing of a mutual recognition agreement in June 1988. Soviet officials claimed that the CMEA-EC agreement lent substance to the concept of the common European home and hoped that it would facilitate Soviet and East European access to Western trade and technology.

The new Soviet willingness to deal with the Community as a "political" entity also reflected an assessment that the Community, while by no means ideal from the Soviet perspective, was less objectionable than certain potentially more dangerous subgroupings such as the long-dormant, but now reviving West European Union (WEU) and the Franco-German relationship. The "Single European Act" of 1985 and the commitment to the establishment of a completely open market in the EC by the end of 1992 also heightened Soviet interest in a new relationship with the Community. In addition to fostering the CMEA-EC link, the Soviet Union began, in January 1987, to negotiate its own bilateral trade and cooperation agreement with the Commission. (The agreement was concluded in December 1989.)

The other new multilateral departure came in the area of conventional arms control. As noted, in his April 1986 speech in East Berlin, Gorbachev proposed sweeping conventional force reductions in the entire Atlantic-to-the-Urals region, and other Soviet officials later suggested that the new proposals could be negotiated at the Stockholm Conference on Disarmament in Europe (CDE) or another CSCE-related forum. The offer to negotiate in an all-European framework represented a dramatic shift from Brezhnev-era positions. In the CSCE negotiations of 1973-1975, the Soviet side had tried to exempt all of Soviet territory from the confidence-building measures under discussion on the grounds that American territory would not be affected and that the Soviet Union could not be accorded a status unequal to that granted the United States. This demand was unacceptable to some European delegations, which argued that the Soviet Union could not invoke its right to equality vis-à-vis the United States to assert in effect an unequal status in Europe. After prolonged negotiations, the sides agreed on a compromise (and, in any case, voluntary) confidence-building regime that included some but exempted the vast majority of the Soviet Union's European territory.

In 1978 when France put forward its proposal for a two-stage European disarmament conference, the Soviets went along in principle, but remained unenthusiastic about extending conventional arms control to their own territory. In the negotiations at Madrid concerning a mandate for the CDE as well as in the early stages of the CDE itself, the Soviets tried either to exclude their own territory or to include the United States by extending the mandatory confidence- and security- building measures to North America or parts of the Atlantic. But in September 1986, the Gorbachev leadership agreed to go along with an "Atlantic-to-the-Urals" confidence-building regime. The CDE agreement thus was important in establishing a precedent for arms control agreements that applied to the breadth of the Soviet Union's European territory (while exempting North America and the high seas).

Throughout 1987, Gorbachev displayed a growing enthusiasm for conventional arms reductions in Europe. In February 1987, he suggested to an international forum in Moscow that military imbalances should be redressed by having the side with superiority in a given category scale down to the level of the other side. Soviet officials also began to acknowledge "asymmetries" in the NATO–WTO balance, some of which favored the East. In the same month, the 23 members of the two alliances began informal consultations aimed at drawing up a mandate for a new bloc-to-bloc arms control forum that would be loosely linked to CSCE. At its May 1987 meeting, the Warsaw Pact's Political Consultative Committee adopted a "Document on the Military Doctrine of the Warsaw Pact States" declaring that Pact military doctrine was purely defensive and that henceforth the Pact would strive to maintain an East-West military balance at the lowest possible level.

Considerable skepticism remained in the West about whether the Soviet Union was in fact prepared to negotiate away its conventional superiority in Europe. In any case, throughout 1987, the diplomatic focus was on nuclear weapons and completion of the INF agreement. But in the summer of 1988—shortly after the U.S. Senate ratification of the INF treaty and the Reagan visit to Moscow—the Soviet authorities apparently made a decision in principle to cut unilaterally their conventional forces and their deployments in Eastern Europe. Gorbachev announced the cuts, which totaled some 500,000 troops, in a speech to the United Nations General Assembly in New York in December, thereby creating a favorable atmosphere for the CFE talks that were expected to convene early the next year.

By late 1988, the focus of Soviet policy had shifted markedly toward Europe as the Reagan-Bush transition resulted in a slowing of U.S.-Soviet negotiations and as breakthroughs in the "all-European process" accelerated. In January, the Vienna CSCE follow-up conference concluded with the signature of a sweeping final document containing unprecedented human rights provisions. The Vienna meeting also produced a mandate for the long-awaited CFE talks, which were scheduled to begin in March. In his speeches to the January and March meetings, Shevardnadze called for steps to overcome the division of Europe and reaffirmed the proclaimed Soviet objectives of ending any foreign military presence in Europe and denuclearizing the continent. Gorbachev visits to Britain, West Germany, France, Italy, and Finland were scheduled in what Soviet commentators would later refer to as the "year of Europe."

The culmination of this phase of Soviet policy was the full normalization of Soviet-West German relations that took place in June 1989 with Gorbachev's visit to Bonn and several other German cities. The visit restored West Germany to its status as the Soviet Union's preferred interlocutor in Western Europe and resulted in numerous agreements, the most important of which was a joint declaration that endorsed key Soviet slogans such as the new political thinking.

The West German public gave the Soviet leader a euphoric welcome, causing unease in other European capitals. At the same time, it appeared that Gorbachev's readiness to take risks to achieve an INF agreement had paid off, as a genuine denuclearization dynamic—helped along by Soviet moves in the conventional field—appeared to gather momentum. The West German government revolted against a NATO plan to proceed with the modernization of Lance missiles. West Germany further insisted on immediate negotiations on nuclear weapons with ranges of less than 500 kilometers (or approximately 300 miles). The U.S.- (and U.K.-) West German dispute was papered over at the May 1989 NATO summit, but pressures for further cuts in NATO nuclear forces were expected to grow.

A month after the visit to West Germany, Gorbachev traveled to France, where he delivered his Strasbourg speech in which he outlined a vision for Europe that included continental transportation and communications projects, a long-term continental ecological program, and other cooperative measures. He also reiterated the call for the elimination of nuclear weapons, but in a shift from previous positions suggested that the Soviet Union could accept temporarily an arms reduction agreement based on the concept of minimal deterrence.

Thus, by the summer of 1989, it appeared that Gorbachev had begun to make significant headway toward realizing his vision of a common European home. This gave rise to a certain ambivalence on the part of many in Western Europe and the United States. The Soviet military threat to Western Europe was diminishing, and the Soviet Union itself was moving toward political pluralism, as was seen most dramatically in the contested elections to the Congress of People's Deputies and the convening of a new Supreme Soviet in the spring of 1989. Soviet officials also began to stress that the Brezhnev Doctrine was dead and that the East European countries were free to decide their own internal affairs. It was unclear how much the Soviet Union was prepared to tolerate in Eastern Europe, but the evidence was mounting that the new limits would be far broader than had been the case in the past.

On the other hand, there were signs of erosion on the Western side that were worrisome to many still concerned about the long-term Soviet threat. NATO nuclear modernization had become extremely problematic, and many concluded that West Germany was well on its way toward effective denuclearization. Gorbachev's enormous popularity with the West European, and especially West German, public promised to complicate NATO efforts to revise conventional planning. And although Gorbachev and other Soviet representatives insisted that the Soviet Union was not interested in eliminating the American presence in Europe, the intended effect of many Soviet proposals seemed to be to undercut the U.S. role.

VII

From the Soviet perspective, there remained but one large cloud on the horizon: Eastern Europe. In June, the Polish Communists suffered a stunning electoral defeat, while in May the Hungarians took the unprecedented step of fully opening their border with Austria. These developments and other rumblings prompted Gorbachev to warn in his Strasbourg speech that it was mistaken to believe that "the overcoming of the division of Europe is the overcoming of socialism." This, he declared, would be "a course for confrontation." Despite these harsh words, Gorbachev and his advisers on balance appeared to believe that change in Eastern Europe could be managed and that the development of a socialist pluralism would contribute to, rather than undermine, the common European home, as well as bolster the reform process in the Soviet Union itself.[6] How wrong these assumptions were soon became obvious.

Most important, Soviet leaders appear to have misunderstood, until it was too late, how inseparably linked were the division of Europe and the division of Germany. With the upheavals in Eastern Europe that began with the refugee crisis at West German embassies throughout the bloc in the late summer, German reunification increasingly emerged as the central issue in Soviet-West European relations. Official support for reunification was an irritant in Soviet-West German relations throughout the 1980s, but one that must have appeared under control to Gorbachev when he made his June 1989 trip to the Federal Republic. During his first several years in power, Gorbachev took a rather hard line on this issue, insisting that it was "closed" and that the European political order and borders were immutable.

As Soviet-West German relations warmed in 1988 and 1989, however, Gorbachev was increasingly exposed to West German critics who argued that he was attempting to create a common European home with a divided Germany at its center. In response to these complaints, Gorbachev modified his stance somewhat. He ceased portraying the division as a permanent and desirable feature of the European order and began to claim that "history" would decide the ultimate fate of the German nation. This helped to defuse a contentious issue that otherwise would have cast a pall over the 1989 summit without really giving away anything concrete. It also sent a not-so-subtle message to the West Germans: If they were really interested in reunification, their best option was to join with the Soviet Union in helping to create the common European home. The German question then could be revisited in a different form at some point in the future.

Gorbachev had reason to believe that this approach to the

---

6. For a discussion of Soviet policy in Eastern Europe before, during, and after the revolutions of 1989, see the contribution of Anne Henderson to this volume.

German question would be effective. There had long been a certain objective convergence between the West German aspiration for a "European peace order" and the Soviet notion of an all-European security system and its newer incarnation, the common European home. This convergence was most apparent during Gorbachev's June visit, when both concepts were endorsed and used almost interchangeably in the joint statement signed by Gorbachev and Kohl.

Within months, however, the Soviet leadership was shocked to learn that the elaborate parallelism between German unity and the European peace order that had figured in hundreds of official German statements over the years was in fact contrived and could be quickly jettisoned when it no longer served German interests. When East Germany began to collapse, Chancellor Kohl and Foreign Minister Genscher suddenly abandoned their rhetoric of previous years and called for very rapid reunification. The end of the division of Germany would no longer come after the construction of a common European home, but would precede it, while creation of a united Europe would remain a distant and very long-term prospect. Still worse, from the Soviet perspective, East Germany's absorption into West Germany meant that the ultimate form of the united Europe would be decided in the West—a complete reversal of Gorbachev's preferred scenario in which he would be the chief architect and sponsor of the common European home.

To some extent, Gorbachev brought the collapse of the German Democratic Republic (GDR) upon himself. In the fall of 1989, he made no secret of his unhappiness with Erich Honecker's government, which had resisted his calls for change and may even have tried to collude with Gorbachev's own domestic opponents. He evidently hoped that Honecker would be replaced by a reform Communist and even helped to precipitate Honecker's fall by his disparaging remarks at the October 1989 fortieth anniversary celebrations in East Berlin. But this attempt to promote East German *perestroika* quickly backfired. Popular pressure for change persisted, leading the authorities to open the Berlin Wall. This in turn led to the virtual collapse of the East German state. The population turned against reform communism (and the various "pink-green" alternatives widely discussed in late 1989), swept away the governments of Egon Krenz and Hans Modrow, and began calling for rapid reunification.

The Soviet response was to try to marshall external support for the survival of a separate East German state. In meetings with Mitterrand and Thatcher (and in talks with the Poles) Gorbachev, Shevardnadze, and other Soviet officials attempted to associate as many states as possible with a go-slow or negative approach to reunification. Gorbachev's call for a "Helsinki II" summit also appeared motivated by a desire to fix the signature of an East German head of state on an authoritative European document. But these efforts failed. Governments in Western and Eastern Europe and especially the United States were wary of being maneuvered into an anti-reunification stance by the Soviet Union.

By February 1990, both the external and internal props of the East German state had collapsed. Gorbachev then accepted the inevitable and agreed, at the Ottawa Open Skies conference, to the "two plus four" formula for talks on reunification that left it to the two German governments to settle the internal terms and included the four postwar occupying powers only in the negotiations on the external aspects. As the talks began, Soviet officials put forward a long list of demands that they claimed were essential to guaranteeing Soviet security and stability in Europe. After initially insisting that Germany become neutral, they proposed that it become a member of both alliances. They also demanded assurances regarding the Polish-German and other borders, the level of German forces, and compensation for the disruption of Soviet-East German trade and economic cooperation.

A major Soviet objective through the late winter and spring 1990 was to slow the process of reunification and thereby to restore a connection between it and the "all European process." As Gorbachev told *Pravda* in February, "history has started working in an unexpectedly rapid way . . . . [I]t follows that the process of the unification of Germany is organically linked with the all-European process and its pivotal line, the formation of a structure of European security that is new in principle and that will replace that which is based upon blocs."

"Synchronization" thus became a major theme in Soviet policy toward Europe, as the Soviet Union attempted not only to slow the process of unification, but also to speed the building of an all-European system. Shevardnadze had already outlined the elements of such a system in his Brussels speech in December 1989 and expanded upon his vision in speeches, interviews, and articles throughout 1990. He called for the establishment of a permanent CSCE secretariat, for annual or biannual meetings of the CSCE foreign ministers, for regular CSCE summits, and for the incorporation of the two alliances into an all-European security structure that in time would absorb their functions and render them obsolete.

IX

In the West, there has always been enormous intellectual resistance to the idea that the Soviet Union ever really wanted to eliminate the American military presence from Europe or that, in light of the developments of the past year, it would desire to do so in the future. Nonetheless, as late as June 1990, Shevardnadze was still promoting a plan that called for the eventual denuclearization of Europe and the simultaneous and phased withdrawal of American and Soviet troops from Germany. But the Soviet Union did not have the negotiating leverage to achieve this kind of settlement, as was seen in July 1990 when Gorbachev finally dropped his objection to the reunification of Germany within NATO.

The outlook for the Soviet Union as a European power, therefore, is mixed. It is unlikely that it will be "expelled" from Europe as many Soviet commentators now fear or profess to fear. Soviet Russia is tied to Europe by numerous bilateral, multilateral, and all-European links, and there is a strong proclivity on the part of Western policymakers to concede that the Soviet

Union has a legitimate claim to "influence" on the continent. On the other hand, it is doubtful that the Soviet Union soon will restore its influence in Europe to what it was throughout most of the postwar period. Moscow now is free of the economic and political burdens of maintaining an exclusive sphere of influence in Eastern Europe, but it can no longer mobilize its own "camp" in all-European forums such as CSCE and CFE.

There also has been a decisive shift in the relative power of Germany and the Soviet Union. Militarily, the Soviet Union probably will retain its traditional advantages. Germany is likely to remain a non-nuclear state and in July 1990, pledged to limit the future size of the *Bundeswehr* to 370,000. But clearly the potential for a stronger German military exists and is bound to raise deep concerns in Moscow. Politically and economically, the shift in the German-Soviet balance is even more pronounced. With the demise of East Germany, the Soviet Union has lost its direct voice in internal German affairs, and some economists are predicting that by 2000 the gross national product (GNP) of a united Germany will surpass that of the Soviet Union.

In the long run, the Soviet Union's status as a European power is likely to be affected less by foreign policy decisions than by how successful it is in dealing with its two most severe internal crises: the economy and the nationalities problem. Deputy Prime Minister Leonid Abalkin has told Soviet audiences that unless the USSR moves quickly toward a real economic reform, "the country has no future as a great power." Movements in various republics (including the Russian Republic's drive for autonomy) may present an even greater challenge to the long-term viability of the Soviet state. The use of force against independence movements would alienate Gorbachev's supporters in the West and shift the balance of power in the Soviet Union to those most opposed to the very reforms needed to integrate the Soviet Union into Europe. On the other hand, if Lithuania and other republics succeed in breaking away, the Soviet Union will suffer blows to its prestige as well as lose those parts of its territory that traditionally have had the closest links with Europe. Thus, although it is unlikely that the Soviet Union will be excluded from influence in Europe by the policies of other powers, its economic and nationalities crises could in time lead to a form of self-exclusion, as the Soviet Union is forced to grapple alone with problems that the rest of Europe may be leaving behind.

II

New Realities in Eastern Europe: Challenges for Russia and the West

Anne Henderson

I T IS THE FATE OF SMALL STATES in the world system that their foreign relations and even domestic structures are more often shaped by external circumstance than by internal choice. This has certainly been the case in Eastern Europe, a region whose experience has been one of domination by a succession of foreign empires. Yet the events of 1989, which freed the nations of Eastern Europe from overt foreign domination, have created possibilities for political and economic self-determination that are unprecedented in their history.

Self-determination, even for great states, never implies complete freedom from external influence. And for the Eastern European nations, even in the most favorable circumstances, independence and autonomy must remain highly qualified. None of these states can afford to sever completely the ties that once bound them to the Soviet Union; the realities of geographical proximity and economic interdependence will perpetuate relations with the USSR even in the absence of military coercion. Nor will the East European nations prove immune to pressure and influence from the Western powers, whose assistance they now seek. Indeed, some observers both in and out of Eastern Europe fear that in their rush to the West the newly liberated countries will simply replace one form of subjugation with another, becoming a group of dependent, backward, and troublesome Western satellites. This view may be simplistic and exaggerated, yet it does point to an important vulnerability.

The author would like to thank Wolfgang Reinicke for his comments on an earlier version of this essay, as well as David Head for his invaluable assistance in preparing the final version.

Situated between a declining superpower and an ascendant European Community, the future of the weak, resource-poor nations of Eastern Europe inevitably will depend on how they manage their relations with the economically and militarily more powerful countries to both their east and west.

Yet more than the fate of Eastern Europe is involved; the fundamental interests of the Soviet Union and the Western nations will also be affected by the region's evolution. Most analysts and policymakers have already recognized that the changes in Eastern Europe will profoundly influence the evolution of East-West relations. But, until recently, the impact of these changes was viewed mainly from a security perspective: Speculation revolved around how the events in Eastern Europe would affect the military balance between the Soviet Union and the West. In the future, however, the economic and political implications of the East European revolutions will overshadow the military dimension in importance. The question of whether the events in Eastern Europe will lead to the end of the Cold War has already been answered. Now the central question is how the events in Eastern Europe will affect the economic and political evolution of the European continent. Successful implementation of liberalizing reforms in Eastern Europe would expedite the long-term goal of constructing a common European house dedicated to enhancing the political stability and economic prosperity of its inhabitants. But the failure of these reforms would endanger the progress toward integrating the Eastern bloc into the world economy and the community of nations, an outcome that would seriously compromise the geopolitical and economic interests of the Western nations.

With so much hanging in the balance, it is clear that the ongoing transformations in Eastern Europe pose serious dilemmas for the Soviet Union, the Western allies, and the Eastern Europeans themselves. The Soviet Union faces, among others, the challenge of dismantling its remaining military controls over Eastern Europe without foreclosing the possibility for future economic and political cooperation with the region. The East European nations confront the dilemma of exploiting their

newfound independence without unleashing forces of destabilizing change that have been constrained by 40 years of Soviet
domination. And the Western allies face the difficult task of
using their new leverage in Eastern Europe to foster stable
liberalization rather than disintegration or repression.

II

The events of the past year cannot be understood without
analyzing the dramatic shift in Soviet strategy toward Eastern
Europe that has occurred during the premiership of Mikhail
Gorbachev. The interests underlying Soviet policy, as well as
the goals of that policy and the extent of Soviet influence in
Eastern Europe, have all changed radically since Gorbachev
came to power. Gorbachev's aim was to reduce the mounting
costs and declining stability of the Soviet Union's East European empire by permitting, and sometimes actively promoting,
increasingly radical reform in the satellite states. His purpose,
in the beginning at least, was to foster an internal evolution
leading to the emergence of states that would be less economically draining and politically dependent upon the Soviet Union.
Yet, the subsequent loosening of Soviet control over Eastern
Europe catalyzed revolutionary changes in the region that
quickly outran the Soviet leadership's original intentions and
desires. By the late fall of 1989, the dilemma confronting the
Soviet Union was clear: Reforms in Eastern Europe were giving
way to revolutions that posed a fundamental threat to Soviet
influence. The only alternative to a profound loss of control, it
appeared, would be a massive application of force. The Soviet
leadership's rejection of military intervention reflected its realization that the use of force would jeopardize Gorbachev's
entire program of domestic reform and foreign relations.

Today, the Soviet Union's goal is no longer to promote
limited reform in Eastern Europe, but rather to avoid total loss
of influence. And the Soviet Union's strategy is no longer an
important catalyst to change in Eastern Europe; instead, it is a
reflexive reaction to events that are transpiring beyond its

control. In assessing the developments in Soviet-East European relations during the past few years, one question assumes central importance: What dramatic shifts in Soviet strategy made it possible to allow these events to take place?

In the era preceding Gorbachev's assumption of power, Eastern Europe served several critical functions for the Soviet Union. Most fundamentally, of course, Eastern Europe provided a security buffer protecting the Soviet Union from the threat of Western aggression. In addition, Eastern Europe constituted a unified bloc of support for Soviet foreign policy in the international arena. Finally, the countries of the region were a source of innovation for the Soviet Union, providing a conduit for the eastward flow of Western technology and serving as an experimental laboratory for reforms that might later be adopted by the Soviets themselves.

Almost as important to the pre-Gorbachev Soviet leadership as the benefits derived from control over Eastern Europe were the fears raised by the prospect of its loss. Soviet leaders realized that loss of control over Eastern Europe would weaken the Soviet Union's leadership role in the socialist world, and undermine the credibility of its doctrine of the irreversibility of socialist revolutions. Equally significant was the fear that loss of control could lead to upheavals in Eastern Europe that would endanger Soviet security and catalyze demands for national autonomy within the Soviet Union itself. In short, the postwar Soviet leadership was convinced that to relinquish its empire would be to risk the collapse of East European regimes, the discrediting of socialism, the loss of secure borders, and the emergence of internal unrest within the Soviet Union.

To maintain its control over Eastern Europe, the Soviet Union traditionally relied on three mechanisms of domination: military coercion, economic pressure, and political linkages. Soviet military strength was used to dominate Eastern Europe not only through occasional invasions, but also through the constant presence of the Warsaw Pact military network. Meanwhile, economic pressure was exerted by exploiting Eastern Europe's dependence upon Soviet raw materials and energy—

the Soviets provided trade benefits as rewards for following Soviet policy prescriptions and withheld supplies to punish defiance of Soviet preferences. Finally, the Soviet Union maintained control over Eastern Europe through the linkages that connected the Communist Party of the Soviet Union (CPSU) to the ruling parties of Eastern Europe. Through a process of consultation with national party leaders, conducted according to the principles of Soviet-imposed democratic centralism, the Soviet Union was able to exert considerable influence over the policy-making process in Eastern Europe.

Although the instruments of Soviet control over Eastern Europe remained the same throughout the postwar period, both the extent and the form of Soviet influence varied widely over time, subject always to the limiting condition that any experimentation be compatible with the basic goal of continued Soviet control. While the Stalinist period was one of thorough-going Soviet domination over Eastern Europe, the late 1950s and early 1960s were marked by increased Soviet toleration of economic and political experimentation within the bloc. After the Czech events of 1968, Soviet toleration for political experiments was sharply reduced, but the Soviet Union did continue to sanction limited economic reforms and growing reliance on Western trade and credits in Eastern Europe. Soviet leaders hoped that these economic changes would bolster East European growth rates, thereby enhancing stability and relieving pressures for political reform.

Yet, increased economic contacts with the West eventually undermined East European stability more than they enhanced it. Most East European governments utilized Western credits to finance imports and consumption, rather than fund investment to generate hard currency exports, a pattern of borrowing that ultimately proved unsustainable. The moment of reckoning came when first Poland, then other East European countries encountered serious debt repayment difficulties in 1981. These difficulties were compounded by rising world interest rates and import prices. When combined with the inefficiencies and distortions inherent in the centrally planned economies of Eastern Europe, the external shocks gave rise to severe economic dislocations in most East European countries by the early 1980s.

In fact, the external shocks of the early 1980s simply exposed and magnified the internal ills that had been afflicting the Eastern European economies for more than a decade. Both labor and capital productivity, and with them overall growth, had been declining inexorably in most East European countries since the early 1970s. These worrisome trends reflected a legacy of entrenched structural economic problems including monopolistic and overly concentrated production facilities, excessive emphasis on anachronistic heavy industries, pervasive subsidization of inefficient firms, distorted and irrational centrally determined price systems, bloated planning bureaucracies, and resource and investment distribution systems that were incapable of responding to market signals or allocating resources to the most productive and efficient users. These structural distortions were reinforced by the behavior of bureaucrats, managers, and workers, who were encouraged by the nature of their systems to waste inputs, hoard resources, overinvest, and seek subsidies rather than profits.

Encumbered by inefficient industrial sectors, anachronistic technology, eroding infrastructure, immense government budget deficits, and stifling external debt burdens, Eastern Europe's stagnation slid toward crisis throughout the 1980s. The economic downturn had ominous political implications. In the past, East European regimes had purchased the grudging toleration of their populations by providing steady growth in production and living standards. But by the 1980s, they were running out of resources to buy popular support.

III

Eastern Europe's interrelated economic and political difficulties contributed to an emerging perception of crisis among the Soviet leadership. Although the Soviet military presence and economic assistance had maintained stability in Eastern Europe in the past, the large costs of this fragile, artificial order were becoming obvious even to the Soviets themselves. However, in the twilight years of the Brezhnev era, and during the brief tenures of Konstantin Chernenko and Yuri Andropov, the Soviet leadership failed to produce any coherent response to the East European problem. Only after Gorbachev's ascension to power in 1985 did the Soviets turn to the task of defining a strategy to avert crisis in Eastern Europe.

The Soviet leadership under Gorbachev confronted two diametrically opposed alternatives. The Soviet Union could tighten its control over Eastern Europe in an effort to suppress mounting pressures for change. Or, it could loosen its grip over Eastern Europe in the hopes that the Communist regimes would utilize their increased autonomy to create viable strategies of economic recovery and political legitimization. After some equivocation in the first two years of Gorbachev's tenure, the Soviet leadership made the fateful decision in 1987 to pursue the second option, as Gorbachev began to emphasize the independence of each Communist party and its "sovereign right to decide the issues facing its country." The decision to permit greater autonomy within the Eastern bloc was motivated by three fundamental considerations: one economic, one military, and one political. Economically, the Soviet Union found the costs of sustaining its empire increasingly burdensome; militarily, it realized that continued control over Eastern Europe was incompatible with its broader strategy of reducing armed confrontation with the West; politically, it acknowledged that the existing regimes in Eastern Europe were illegitimate, corrupt, and incapable of solving their nations' pressing problems.

One of the most important motivations underlying the shift in Soviet strategy was the growing cost of controlling Eastern Europe through traditional military and economic mechanisms. The Soviet Union, which financed 80 percent of Warsaw Pact expenditures, felt that the expense of maintaining a huge military organization in Eastern Europe was severely straining Soviet resources. In addition, Soviet economic relations with

Eastern Europe were increasingly viewed as disadvantageous. Since the first postwar decade, the Soviet Union had subsidized Eastern Europe through the provision of cheap raw materials and energy and the purchase of substandard Eastern European exports at inflated prices. According to one estimate, Soviet subsidization of Eastern Europe increased from less than $250 million a year in the early 1960s to more than $10 billion a year in the early 1980s.[1] The military and economic costs of empire imposed unsustainable demands upon the already enfeebled Soviet economy and led Gorbachev to the conclusion that Russian economic recovery depended upon ridding the USSR of the encumbrance of Eastern Europe.

This motivating factor was reinforced by a more fundamental shift in Soviet military doctrine under Gorbachev. Impelled above all by a sense of economic decline and a mounting fear of long-term strategic weakening, the Soviet leadership sought to reverse the escalating arms race, ease the tension between the two antagonistic blocs, and create the preconditions for rapprochement between East and West. Underlying this new set of goals was a revolutionary redefinition of Soviet security interests. In the "new thinking" of Mikhail Gorbachev and his supporters, the main threat to Soviet security was no longer perceived as one of Western military invasion, but rather one of economic breakdown and political destabilization within the Soviet Union itself. As a result, Soviet security interests no longer required the maintenance of a security cordon of tightly controlled East European allies. To the contrary, Soviet security interests could best be served by easing control over Eastern Europe. To convince Western nations to sign arms treaties and commercial agreements that would reduce the Soviet Union's

---

1. The vast increase in subsidization reflected the fact that world market prices for oil rose rapidly after 1973, while the price of Soviet oil and raw material deliveries to Eastern Europe increased much more slowly. See Michael Marrese and Jan Vanous, *Soviet Subsidization of Trade with Eastern Europe: A Soviet Perspective* (Berkeley, Calif: University of California Institute of International Studies, 1983).

unsustainably large military expenditures and provide the economic benefits crucial to Soviet recovery, the USSR had to demonstrate its commitment to loosening control over the Eastern bloc.

The final factor motivating the dramatic shift in Soviet strategy toward Eastern Europe was the inherent fragility of East European regimes kept afloat by Soviet military force and economic subsidization. Gorbachev recognized that his predecessors' policies in Eastern Europe had created political systems that were devoid of domestic support or legitimacy. In essence, the same Soviet power that had maintained the Eastern European regimes throughout the postwar period had also prevented them from making the transition from externally imposed dictatorships to indigenously legitimated governments. As Foreign Minister Eduard Shevardnadze explained, the Soviet leadership recognized that "a cordon sanitaire artificially created around the USSR out of shaky regimes . . . propped up by [Soviet] bayonets" could not be maintained.[2] But this recognition also imposed a dilemma on the Soviet leadership: How could the USSR cut back its military and economic commitments in Eastern Europe without engendering destabilization and total collapse in the region? Gorbachev evidently concluded that the best solution to this dilemma lay in granting substantial independence to the nations of Eastern Europe, thereby allowing Eastern European regimes to legitimize themselves through choosing their own autonomous paths to socialism.

Between 1987 and 1989, accordingly, the Soviet leadership repudiated several key elements in its traditional East European strategy. Most important, the Soviet Union renounced its prerogative to interfere in internal East European politics and called for major reforms in the realm of intrabloc economic and military relations. Yet, the initial shift in strategy should not be

---

2. Foreign Broadcast Information Service (FBIS) Daily Report, Soviet Union, March 16, 1990.

overdrawn; the new policy as originally outlined still exhibited elements of continuity and caution. In terms of East European internal affairs, for example, the Soviet leadership envisioned the *rehabilitation* of socialism along the lines of *glasnost* and *perestroika* in the Soviet Union, but not the *repudiation* of the socialist model. And in the realm of external affairs, the Soviet Union wished to restructure its relations with Eastern Europe without actually dismantling the Council for Mutual Economic Assistance (CMEA) and Warsaw Pact institutions that had allowed it to dominate Eastern Europe militarily and economically for decades. In short, the early Soviet strategy was one of reform, rather than revolution.

The most striking departure from past Soviet policy was the renunciation of the Brezhnev Doctrine, the policy first pronounced in the wake of Soviet invasion of Czechoslovakia in August 1968, which had since served as the Soviet justification for intervention in Eastern Europe. This renunciation, hinted at in 1987–1988, was finally made explicit in Gorbachev's July 1989 speech to the Council of Europe, in which he proclaimed that "any interference in domestic affairs, and any attempts to restrict the sovereignty of states—friends, allies, or others—are inadmissable."

In practical terms, the repudiation of the Brezhnev Doctrine meant that the Soviet leadership's attitude toward economic and political change in Eastern Europe became increasingly permissive. In a striking departure from past Soviet policy, Gorbachev sanctioned political, as well as economic reform initiatives in Eastern Europe in 1987-1989. Gorbachev's support of economic and political experimentation in Eastern Europe appeared to be a logical extension of his domestic program of *glasnost* and *perestroika*. As in the Soviet Union itself, the hope was presumably that liberalizing reforms in Eastern Europe would enhance economic performance, bolster regime legitimacy, and defuse the looming threat of political instability.

The Soviet leadership was almost certainly aware that the link between reform and stability was not necessarily positive:

In the short term, economic liberalization would most likely generate popular unrest over higher prices and increased unemployment, and political liberalization might only fuel this unrest by providing expanded opportunities for its articulation. Partly to avoid exacerbating the potential impact of reform, and partly to give substance to its new doctrine of noninterference, the Soviet leadership did not attempt to force reforms upon Eastern European regimes that rejected the need for change and that seemed capable of maintaining stability without it. So while the Soviet Union sanctioned Polish and Hungarian reform experiments, a discreet official silence was maintained concerning the rigid antireformism of the East German, Bulgarian, Czech, and Romanian regimes.

Yet, the Soviet leadership's official declarations (and private expectations) concerning the internal evolution of Eastern European societies remained rather vague. Gorbachev's stock reply to queries on the future of Eastern Europe was that each nation would be free to pursue its own road to socialism, but that certain overarching principles would continue to bind the socialist countries together. Unfortunately, Gorbachev seemed incapable of specifying these overarching principles. This left the limits of internal change in Eastern Europe rather indeterminate, both in the eyes of Western observers and of the Eastern Europeans themselves. In any event, it is now evident that before the revolutionary upheavals of late 1989, the Soviet Union did not anticipate that the Eastern European nations would take advantage of their new autonomy to repudiate socialism entirely.

IV

In hindsight, the change in Soviet relations with Eastern Europe between 1987 and 1989 can be seen as a bold, yet ultimately ineffective, exercise in crisis avoidance, motivated less by a coherent strategy than by a combination of wishful thinking and economic exhaustion. The cost of maintaining an empire through military coercion and economic aid had become too high, so the Soviet leadership gave way to the hope that somehow diversity and autonomy would provide the stable framework that imposition and subsidization could no longer maintain. The strategy failed, and the pressures for change that had been unleashed by Gorbachev took on an unforeseen and relentless dynamic. Soon after the Soviet controls, which had maintained order in the past, were lifted, Gorbachev's hopes for gradual, limited reform were swamped by a rising tide of demands for revolutionary change.

As the tumultuous events of the fall and winter 1989 unfolded, the Soviet leadership scrambled to define a coherent policy response to the escalating unrest in Eastern Europe. Apparently, the option of using military force to uphold Communist regimes and preserve order was never seriously considered. The Soviet leadership, realizing that efforts to suppress Eastern European insurrections would be both expensive and protracted, was reluctant to give up the hard-won progress in East-West relations achieved during the past four years. Gorbachev, in effect, became a victim of his own policy success—he had gone so far in promoting East European autonomy and courting Western approval that he could not reverse course without dealing a severe blow to his entire domestic and foreign policy program. As Foreign Minister Shevardnadze explained, "What could we do? Send in the troops? Of course, we could start shooting, but then we would have to cross out everything to do with *perestroika* and democratization."[3]

Faced with the demise of their last delusions about Eastern Europe, the Soviet leadership has been forced to rebuild relations with its erstwhile satellite allies on an entirely new basis. Gone are the days when Soviet diplomats could simply convey the CPSU's wishes to its subordinate satellite parties in Eastern Europe; now, Soviet officials are obliged to negotiate with independent new governments headed by ex-dissidents

---

3. FBIS Daily Report, Soviet Union, April 23, 1990.

and fervent anti-Communists who have spent their political lives denouncing Soviet domination. In this radically changed environment, the Soviet leadership has attempted to transform its relations within the CMEA and the Warsaw Pact in a desperate effort to prevent the complete disintegration of these organizations.

The 1990 negotiations over CMEA restructuring were the most conflictual in the organization's history, with some members calling for its complete dissolution and others demanding radical reforms in its operations. The Soviet Union was foremost in urging immediate changes in the CMEA—an understandable position because the Soviet Union bore the greatest economic costs from the existing terms of CMEA trade. In past years, the USSR had been willing to accept shoddy, overpriced Eastern European manufactured goods in return for raw materials that could have been sold for hard currency on world markets. But this sacrifice, once seen as an unavoidable cost of empire, became pointless after 1989; with the collapse of Soviet control over Eastern Europe, the Soviet Union had no more reason to subsidize Hungary than it had to subsidize France or Germany. The Soviet Union was determined to convert the CMEA from a costly, cumbersome instrument of imperial control into a fully functioning economic organization run according to market principles. Paramount among the Soviet Union's demands was that CMEA trade be conducted in convertible currencies at world market prices. This switch would force the East European nations to cut the prices of many of their exports to the USSR and cause them to pay more in valuable hard currency (rather than in worthless transferable rubles) for Soviet imports.

Several East European countries were dismayed by the Soviet proposals. Reducing the inflated prices of East European exports would devastate the region's manufacturing sectors; requiring payment in convertible currency would cause a catastrophic drain on Eastern European hard currency reserves; and the new trade rules would reduce East European purchasing power vis-à-vis the Soviet Union by 30 percent, leaving

Eastern Europe with a $10 billion trade deficit.[4] Given their already severe economic crises—which they attributed to 40 years of Soviet-imposed economic planning—the Eastern European countries were not eager to provide costly trade concessions to their former imperial oppressors. Although they agreed that the CMEA must undergo market-oriented restructuring to survive, they called for a more gradual transition to convertible currency trade than the Soviet Union proposed.

In the past, the outcome of this conflict would have been predictable. The Soviet Union dominated the CMEA before 1989 and regularly pushed through its policy proposals over East European objections. But the political ties that formerly held the East European governments in thrall had been severed, and the economic rewards that the Soviet Union had previously used as inducements for Eastern European compliance were now being withdrawn at the Soviet Union's own initiative. As the East European delegates to the January 1990 CMEA conference warned, the Soviet Union must relinquish its position of dominance within the CMEA or else risk wholesale Eastern European defection from the organization.

In fact, however, neither the Soviet Union nor the countries of Eastern Europe can afford to abandon the CMEA. As Czech Foreign Trade Minister Andrej Barcak admitted, "You don't walk out of your home if you have no other home to move into." With acceptance into the European Economic Community impossible in the short term, the Soviet Union and the East European countries can hardly forsake the trading system that provides them with guaranteed access to crucial products and materials: The Soviet Union relies heavily on East European manufactured goods, and Eastern Europe obtains almost all of its energy from the USSR. In such a situation of interdependence, compromise is necessary, and during the first half of 1990, the Soviets and East Europeans

---

4. Figures provided by PlanEcon, Washington DC, January 1990.

moved toward a modus vivendi in their trade relationships. Several East European countries signed agreements with the Soviet Union to convert trade to convertible currencies at world market prices. In return, the Soviet Union has promised to maintain its raw material deliveries to Eastern Europe rather than reorient exports to Western markets.

Nevertheless, the transition to a viable, market-oriented CMEA will be a long and difficult process with limited prospects for success. Although the East European states and the Soviet Union agree that CMEA trade must be converted from the basis of centrally planned government delivery contracts to independent market transactions between individual firms, the wide disparities in the pace of economic reform among the CMEA countries make a rapid switch impossible. Instead, the CMEA will likely remain mired in a cumbersome and debilitating transition phase, with the more advanced reformers (Hungary and Poland) seeking greener economic pastures in Western markets, and the laggards squabbling over the division of the remaining scraps within the CMEA.

Although the Soviet Union has put priority on restructuring intrabloc economic relations, it now also places considerable emphasis on transforming Eastern Europe's economic relations with the West. After decades of regarding these with apprehension, the Soviet Union has abandoned its traditional qualms and begun to promote East-West economic integration wholeheartedly. This departure marks a belated Soviet realization that the only hope for Eastern Europe's economic recovery lays in the vigorous pursuit of Western markets, technology, trade, and investment. Naturally, Soviet requests for Western economic assistance to Eastern Europe have been motivated less by altruistic concern for the economic health of its former satellites than by self-interest. The Soviets hope that Western joint ventures, credits, and investments will provide the resource infusions necessary to shore up East European economies and eliminate the need for Soviet assistance.

V

As the mutual security interests that united the members of the Warsaw Pact and NATO lose potency and as the economic interactions between the two blocs intensify, traditionally dominant military and security concerns will be eclipsed by political and economic considerations as the focal point of East-West relations. Looking to the future, the central issue regarding Eastern Europe's security status is not what role Eastern Europe will play in the Warsaw Pact itself, but rather what role it will play in the Warsaw Pact's disintegration. Given the Soviet Union's decision to remove its troops from most of Eastern Europe and in view of the fact that some East European governments are considering or have announced plans to withdraw from the Warsaw Pact entirely, the WTO has already lost credibility as a functioning military alliance. German reunification within NATO by the end of 1990 will seal the fate of the Warsaw Treaty Organization.

Soviet officials are among the first to acknowledge that the Warsaw Pact has no real future. For them, no less than for everyone else, the question is not whether, but when and how the alliance should be dissolved. The long-term objective, Soviet leaders argue, should be the simultaneous dissolution of the Western and Eastern alliances into an overarching pan-European defense order. However, they appear determined to prevent the immediate disintegration of the WTO, whose continued existence is seen as necessary to maintain Soviet security and European stability during the transition to a joint East-West security system. Thus far, the Soviet Union's position on the Warsaw Pact has reflected two intertwined strategic and economic goals: to prevent East European defections from the Pact and to reduce overall levels of conventional forces in Europe.

As part of its effort to achieve these goals, the Soviet Union has proclaimed a thorough transformation in the Warsaw Pact's structure and functions. With an eye to reassuring the East Europeans, it has renounced the legacy of a Soviet-dominated alliance that feared internal nonconformity almost as much as external aggression. Instead, the Soviet Union promises a flexible and pluralistic alliance "based upon the authentic and not just the formal equality of its members," within which all countries can pursue both national goals and mutual interests.[5] The Soviet leadership has also tried to convince Eastern Europe that the Warsaw Pact can restructure itself from a military alliance to a "socioeconomic" association charged with carrying out a common strategy to overcome the backwardness of the Eastern bloc. Meanwhile, the Soviets have tried to convince the Western nations that the Warsaw Pact can transform itself from an antagonist to an ally, which would cooperate with NATO to reduce armaments and strengthen global security.

The Soviet Union's efforts to salvage the Warsaw Pact through redefining its raison d'être are unlikely to succeed. The Warsaw Pact is certainly changing, but in the direction of dissolution rather than renewal. The most concrete manifestation of this process is the ongoing unilateral troop withdrawal from Eastern Europe. In February 1990, the Soviet Union made a dramatic concession at the Vienna Conventional Arms talks by agreeing to reduce its European troop strength levels below those maintained by NATO. This concession was the product of both economic and political imperatives: The ailing Soviet economy could no longer sustain the burden of massive conventional arms spending, and several new East European governments simply refused to allow Soviet troops to remain on their soil. At the insistence of the Hungarian and Czech governments, the Soviet Union agreed to pull out all its forces from their countries by mid-1991; several top Polish officials have called for Soviet troop withdrawals as well. This leaves only the Soviet forces in what is currently East Germany as the sole outpost of Warsaw Pact forces in Europe, and their

---

5. Interview with V.P. Karpov, deputy foreign minister, *Komsomolskaya Pravda*, December 20, 1989, p. 3.

continued presence after reunification would be problematic, to say the very least.

If the military capacity of the Warsaw Pact has been severely attenuated, its political rationale has all but disappeared. The process of democratization within the Pact has revealed more conflicting perspectives than common interests. At the March and June 1990 Warsaw Pact summits, for example, members disagreed strongly on the issue of German reunification, and the summit broke up without formulating a common position. Meanwhile, most East European governments are coming under increasing popular pressure to sever their military ties with the Soviet Union. Particularly in Hungary, Poland, and Czechoslovakia, incumbent governments have been barraged with complaints about their perceived timidity in dealing with the Soviet Union. Demonstrations have been held denouncing the slow pace of Soviet troop pullouts, and opposition parties have sought to capitalize on this public sentiment by demanding total withdrawal from the Warsaw Pact. Inevitably, the new realities of democratic politics will force East European governments to respond to the increasingly intense popular resentment of Soviet military obligations.

It is unclear what inducements the Soviets can offer to keep the countries of Eastern Europe in the Warsaw Pact. Two of the three traditional instruments of Soviet influence over Eastern Europe—military force and political pressure—have been fundamentally weakened, if not entirely eliminated since 1989. And the third traditional mechanism—economic leverage—will retain its effectiveness only as long as the Soviet Union continues to offer its invaluable energy resources to Eastern Europe on concessionary terms. Because the Soviet Union has announced its intention of converting its economic relations with Eastern Europe to a strictly commercial basis, it will soon lose much of its power to either bribe or threaten Eastern Europe through the mechanism of trade.

The fundamental and inexorable weakening of the USSR's influence in its relations with Eastern Europe is most dramatically revealed in the evolution of the Soviet stance on German reunification. In its initial reaction to the collapse of the Honecker regime, the Soviet Union reiterated its traditional opposition to German reunification, insisting that the division of Germany into two separate states belonging to two different security alliances was necessary to maintain balance and stability in Europe. Then, by the end of 1989, Gorbachev and other Soviet leaders had acknowledged the inevitability of reunification and began to pursue the fallback goal of keeping a unified Germany out of NATO. However, the Soviet Union lacked sufficient bargaining leverage to outmaneuver the Western nations in the two-plus-four negotiations, slow the accelerating process of inter-German economic and political union, or arrest East Germany's trajectory toward assimilation into NATO. With the unified Germany's membership in NATO now assured, the only remaining questions involve the details (including the financial price) of the face-saving compromise, which will permit Germany to remain in NATO without gratuitously humiliating the USSR by forcing an immediate, complete sundering of German relations with the WTO.

Only recently has the Soviet leadership begun to grasp the enormity of the changes that have taken place in Eastern Europe. As an article in *Izvestiia* recently acknowledged, the "socialist camp" no longer exists: "No ideological kinship can be seen with the new governments of Eastern Europe, and nothing but outward diplomatic decorum remains of the Warsaw Pact." In one sense, the collapse of communism in Eastern Europe constitutes a humiliating defeat for the Soviet Union and its Eastern European strategy. When Gorbachev took his first steps away from the Brezhnev Doctrine in 1986-1987, he did not intend to set in motion a process that would culminate in the overthrow of every East European regime, the disintegration of the Warsaw Pact, and through the demonstration effect, the intensification of national separatist sentiment within the Soviet Union itself.

In another sense, however, the collapse of the Soviet empire in Eastern Europe represents a perverse victory for the USSR.

The Soviet Union has managed to rid itself of a perennial economic drain and a political headache. Having dumped the task of ensuring Eastern Europe's economic recovery and political stability into the lap of the Western allies, the Soviet Union is now "free" to deal with its own internal economic and political crises. At the same time, the Soviet leadership's response to the revolutions in Eastern Europe has earned it the respect and trust of many Western governments, increasing their willingness to reach critical arms control agreements with the Soviet Union and to open the doors to liberal trade and even credit.

By accepting the demise of socialism graciously, and discarding their military and economic millstones adroitly, the Soviet leadership may have purchased the time and goodwill needed to pursue internal reform without the burden of superpower competition. If the Soviet Union continues to respond flexibly to change in Eastern Europe, it may be able to overcome the negative legacy of the postwar era and construct a new set of relationships with its East and West European neighbors based on mutual economic and political interests. This would be a development that would benefit all inhabitants of the common European home, not least the Eastern Europeans themselves.

VI

The USSR is not the only country whose national interests have been challenged by developments in Eastern Europe; the countries of the Western alliance have been affected as well, although in a dramatically different fashion. While the dilemmas faced by the Soviets revolve around relinquishing the burdens of empire without destroying the prospects for economic and security cooperation with Eastern Europe, the dilemmas of the West revolve around supporting a stable transition to capitalist democracy in Eastern Europe and integrating Eastern Europe into a common European home. In pursuing these goals, the Western nations should avoid both naive optimism concerning the victory of capitalist democracy in Eastern Europe and suspicious inflexibility concerning the need for a new pan-European security order now that the rationale for maintaining two separate, antagonistic blocs is disappearing.

Since 1989, the United States and its allies have been grappling with the task of formulating policy responses to the dramatic changes taking place in Eastern Europe. In the four preceding decades, the Western allies had maintained that their ultimate goal in Eastern Europe was liberation from Soviet control. But there was never any question of formulating concrete policies to achieve this goal because it appeared completely out of reach. Convinced that challenges to the Soviet domination of Eastern Europe would provoke counterproductive confrontations, the Western nations tacitly accepted Soviet control while publicly denouncing it.

Only after the previously incontrovertible reality of Soviet control over Eastern Europe was brought into question for the first time in the postwar period did the Western nations realize that their minimalist policy could no longer meet the challenges and opportunities of a new era. Yet, the West initially found it difficult to formulate a coherent response to the developments in Eastern Europe. Because of disputes within the Western alliance and because of the inherent caution and incrementalism that characterized the political processes of several Western nations, the NATO countries played only a limited and reactive role in the East European revolutions of 1989.

Yet, the Western nations do have a critical role to play in the period of postrevolutionary consolidation in Eastern Europe. Without Western support, disastrous breakdowns in Eastern European reform experiments are almost inevitable, and the repercussions of such breakdowns would not leave the Western nations unaffected. Western geopolitical interests would hardly be served by the emergence of an unstable, crisis-ridden Eastern Europe prone to outbreaks of ethnic and religious violence and escalating territorial conflicts. Nor would it serve the West's economic interests to be faced with a group of disintegrating East European societies incapable of repaying their huge debt to the West or of preventing a vast westward outflow of disgruntled émigrés. Having already spent trillions of dollars in their postwar efforts to contain communism in Eastern Europe, the Western nations cannot afford to refuse to contribute a few billion more to the process of consolidating democracy in the region.

To confront the challenges and opportunities presented by the recent revolutions in Eastern Europe, the Western nations have begun to redefine the basic goals of their East European strategy, the political and economic scope of that strategy, the specific targets of their policy efforts, and the institutional framework within which policy decisions are reached. In terms of goals, the former objective of preventing communism's external expansion while hastening its internal collapse has been achieved. So the Western nations have turned their attention to a new agenda of consolidating capitalist, Western-oriented democracies in Eastern Europe. The Western nations have expanded dramatically the scope of their East European strategy as well, moving from limited economic and diplomatic contacts to extensive trade, investment, scientific, technical, and diplomatic interactions. Meanwhile, the Western allies have shifted the targets of their East European strategy from a few favored mavericks to the entire Eastern bloc.

Finally, and perhaps most significantly, the Western countries have altered the framework within which they formulate Eastern European policy, from the U.S.-centric NATO arena to a broader and more representative range of organizations, including the EC, the Council of Europe, and the CSCE. At the December 1989 summit, for example, the EC designated itself as the focal point of efforts to build a united Europe: "The Community is the cornerstone of a new European architecture and the mooring for a future European equilibrium." This shift in institutional framework reflects a potentially far-reaching change in the distribution of decision-making power within the Atlantic Alliance. Before 1990, the United States played the dominant role in formulating Western policies toward the

Eastern bloc. But in the past year, the nations of Western Europe have seized the initiative in the realm of East European policy, asserting that the collapse of the bipolar Cold War system warranted a shift in East-West relations in which the continental Europeans would replace the Soviets and the Americans as the main architects of a new European order.

In response to this growing European assertiveness, the United States tacitly ceded its leadership position, motivated by three basic considerations. First, the U.S. government felt little inclination to shoulder a preponderant share of the economic burden of resuscitating Eastern Europe. Second, U.S. officials felt that West European-led initiatives in Eastern Europe would be more palatable to the Soviet Union than American incursions. Finally, the U.S. government wished to avoid the acrimony and humiliation of challenging the West Europeans for the dominant role that they clearly have the economic power and political determination to pursue.

The resulting shift in the distribution of responsibility and power within the Western alliance is not transpiring without conflict—disputes continue to erupt between U.S. and West European leaders and among the Europeans themselves. And there is clearly anxiety on the part of France, Britain, and other nations that Germany will move unilaterally to set up an East European strategy that will consolidate its own economic and diplomatic dominance in the region. Nevertheless, movement toward a European-led Western strategy in Eastern Europe is clearly discernible. The Western allies have embarked on a joint effort to promote capitalist democracy in Eastern Europe to serve their own economic interests, improve East-West relations, and enhance the internal viability of Eastern European societies.

VII

How, specifically, can the Western allies advance the causes of political democratization, economic liberalization, and social stability in Eastern Europe? Already, the Western nations have begun to assess the diplomatic, political, and economic policy instruments at their disposal. They have concluded that diplomatic and political initiatives can be effective in certain circumstances. For example, fuller observance of human rights in Eastern Europe can be encouraged through negotiations in international forums such as the CSCE. In addition, the Western nations are planning to support the development of democratic political systems in Eastern Europe through organizations, such as the volunteer U.S. "Democracy Corps," which will help set up the legal and institutional infrastructure for representative governments.

Yet, the most powerful instruments of Western influence in Eastern Europe are undoubtedly economic. In the final analysis, the West's financial, trade, and technological resources will be most important to the success of economic restructuring and the viability of political reform in Eastern Europe. The nations of Eastern Europe are currently confronting a formidable array of economic and social difficulties. Eastern Europe's economic performance in 1989 was probably the worst since the immediate postwar period—almost every country suffered dramatic declines in output and investment, combined with accelerating inflation and deteriorating trade balances. And in the midst of this severe and continuing crisis, most East European nations are struggling to carry out wrenching changes involving the destruction of entrenched Communist bureaucracies, the restructuring of entire industrial and agricultural sectors, and the transformation of the attitudes of citizens accustomed to secure and unchallenging work environments. These changes entail massive dislocations at a time in which the East European societies are already reeling from the shocks of domestic stagflation and external imbalance.

At this critical juncture, Western economic assistance could prove invaluable in easing the transition from crisis-ridden socialism to stable democracy in Eastern Europe. But the possibility also exists that the transfer of Western resources could have a deleterious, rather than a regenerative, impact upon Eastern Europe. For example, if East European countries were to repeat their past history of waste and misallocation of Western loans, they would face serious debt repayment problems that could catalyze a loss of creditor confidence and a cessation of credit flows. A credit cutoff would, in turn, generate even greater economic difficulties, creating a vicious circle of Western financial withdrawal and East European disintegration.

The Western nations are well aware of the need to devise an effective transfer strategy to avoid a potentially disastrous misuse of resources in Eastern Europe. To this end, the United States has called for the continuation of its traditional quid-pro-quo approach, in which the granting of benefits is contingent upon fulfillment of specific economic or political conditions. In the past, the Western European nations were skeptical about the utility of this linkage approach, believing that Western efforts to force Eastern European policy shifts through sanctions and rewards would prove counterproductive. Since 1989, however, both the prospects and the price tag for employing an economic linkage strategy have risen dramatically, and as a result, the Western Europeans have embraced the need for conditionality to ensure that the re-sources they provide to Eastern Europe are effectively utilized.

There are four basic avenues through which the Western nations can provide economic support for Eastern European reform efforts: credit, trade, investments, and technical assistance. Since 1989, the question of financial credit for Eastern Europe has provoked considerable controversy. The first issue that had to be dealt with was the question of Eastern Europe's existing debt burden. After the revolutions of 1989, Eastern Europe's credit rating plummeted, and bankers predicted that the region would be virtually shut out of international capital markets for years. This was a particularly ominous development for countries such as Hungary, Poland, and Bulgaria, which were incapable of servicing their considerable external debts without an inflow of new resources. The resultant threat of financial collapse has revealed the urgent need for debt relief in Eastern Europe. No successful transition from plan to market can occur while Eastern European economies are being crushed under the weight of enormous debt burdens and while the resources that are urgently needed to fund economic restructuring are being channeled into debt repayment. In fact, full debt repayment is simply incompatible with economic reform and recovery in several Eastern European nations.[6]

So far, the Western nations have made only tentative efforts to resolve the financial dilemmas of the heavily indebted East European countries. In early 1990, the U.S. government called on American banks to write off their Polish debts, while refusing to do the same for its own loans to Poland—a proposal that the commercial banks treated with understandable derision. Slightly more constructive were the subsequent U.S. proposals to provide debt relief to Poland in accordance with the provisions of the Brady Plan and the West German government's decision to forgive $400 million of its loans to Poland. In fact, both Western banks and governments can well afford to provide debt relief to Eastern Europe. The commercial banks have already set aside reserves covering the majority of their outstanding loans in the region, and the Western governments would better serve their own and Eastern European interests by forgiving past loans than by piling new credits on top of already crushing debt burdens. Unfortunately, neither the banks nor the governments have yet reached a comprehensive agreement on East European debt relief.

Meanwhile, the Western nations have had to deal with the issue of nonrepayable financial aid to Eastern Europe. Several analysts have proposed a new Marshall Plan for Eastern Europe, arguing that the economic difficulties that confront postrevolutionary Eastern Europe are strikingly similar to those that faced postwar Western Europe. Eastern Europe in 1990,

---

6. For example, Poland's per capita debt amounts to half its per capita GNP, and if regularly serviced, would absorb 90 percent of its export revenues. Mark Palmer, "U.S. and Western Policy—New Opportunities for Action," in William E. Griffith, ed., *Central and Eastern Europe: The Opening Curtain?* (Boulder, Colo: Westview Press, 1989), 393.

like Western Europe in 1945, suffers from the severe handicaps of outmoded industrial and infrastructural bases in a state of disastrous disrepair, overvalued and nonconvertible currencies, pent-up excess demand for industrial and consumer imports, onerous external debt burdens, and rising popular expectations combined with insufficient public resources. Advocates of an East European Marshall Plan contend that history could repeat itself in Eastern Europe, with donated funds financing economic reconstruction by facilitating essential imports, easing production bottlenecks, and permitting simultaneous increases in investment and consumption. Yet, no concrete proposal for an Eastern European Marshall Plan has been put forward by the Western governments, not so much because of the cost—which would have represented only one-tenth of 1 percent of the Western nations' GNP—but because of fundamental differences in the circumstances of 1945 and 1990. The West European nations of 1945 were resource-poor but market-oriented, capable of highly efficient allocation and utilization of financial assistance. In 1990, by contrast, the distorted command economies of Eastern Europe were incapable of absorbing large resource inflows; they could not employ credits effectively before undertaking fundamental restructuring of their production and investment systems. The Western nations therefore concluded that pouring vast financial resources into East European economies would result in nothing but waste and misallocation.

This rejection of an East European Marshall Plan does not represent a denial of Eastern Europe's urgent need for Western financial assistance. Rather, it reflects the Western nations' determination to ensure that the preconditions for effective resource utilization are fulfilled before the flow of aid commences. Accordingly, the Western nations have begun to provide a wide array of technical assistance to help the Eastern European nations set up the legal and institutional infrastructure of market economies. They have pledged their assistance in setting up investment banks, insurance companies, and securities markets; in improving the quality of Eastern

European statistics; and in developing the marketing and managerial skills needed to help Eastern European enterprises compete in domestic and international markets. The Western nations anticipate that, with the help of their economists, bankers, lawyers, accountants, and management consultants, the countries of Eastern Europe can condense the creation of market economies—a process that took centuries in the West—into a few short years. This will enable the East European economies to absorb Western resources far more efficiently than under the conditions of unreformed central planning.

At the same time that they pledged technical support for the development of market economies, the Western allies undertook a variety of financial initiatives designed to provide conditional assistance to reform-oriented East European regimes. In addition to the funds being channeled through the PHARE initiative of the Group of 24 (which includes the United States, Canada, the members of the European Community [EC] and the European Free Trade Association [EFTA] Turkey, New Zealand, and Australia). Western governments have promised billions of dollars in new credits to finance hard-currency–earning projects to guarantee loans for joint venture investments and to support the transition to currency convertibility.[7] International financial institutions are also becoming involved in the business of financing East European reforms. The International Monetary Fund and the World Bank have provided sizable loans to Hungary and Poland in support of their market-oriented stabilization and adjustment programs. Perhaps most significant, a new European Bank for Reconstruction and Development was founded in 1990, with

---

7. For instance, West Germany has pledged a $2.2 billion assistance program for Poland; France has promised $650 million in trade and investment credits; Japan has announced a $1 billion package of low-interest import credits for Hungary and Poland; and the United States has shifted an incremental $250 million of its $8 billion foreign aid budget for 1990 to Hungary and Poland.

a membership including the United States, the Soviet Union, and the nations of Eastern and Western Europe, an initial capital base of $12 billion, and a mission of stimulating private investment in Eastern Europe.[8] Taken together, the pledges of Western financial assistance for Eastern Europe amount to an impressive total of $17 billion, of which 80 percent has been designated for use by Hungary and Poland.

These diverse forms of Western financial assistance have three common features: They all involve highly conditional credits linked to the implementation of market-oriented reforms; they have all been underwritten mainly by the Western Europeans rather than the United States; and they have all been directed almost exclusively toward the "model" reformist regimes of Hungary and Poland. One of these features—Western Europe's predominant role—will likely be reinforced in the coming decade. But, over time, reforms in Eastern Europe will likely progress to the point where conditional credits for a few favored regimes will be replaced by a less selective and intrusive approach in which all East European nations are accorded the freedom to utilize loans as they see fit. Indeed, the transition to a less restrictive framework for East European financial assistance is already being planned; the European Community is discussing the establishment of a "flexible financing facility" that all Eastern European nations could draw upon freely in support of economic reforms. If and when it occurs, this development will mark the maturation of both Eastern European reform efforts and East-West financial relations.

---

8. At least 60 percent of the Bank's credits have been earmarked for investment in the fledgling East European private sector. The EC nations dominate the EBRD, controlling 51 percent of its quotas and playing a predominant role in its operations.

VIII

Just as critical to Eastern Europe's regeneration as Western credits are Western trade opportunities. Ever since the 1960s, the governments of Eastern Europe have sought to expand their trade relations with the West, realizing that the CMEA was incapable of providing the high-quality, advanced-technology products critical to their nations' economic development. This long-standing quest for Western trading opportunities has acquired added urgency since 1989. The postrevolutionary East European regimes are convinced that the viability of their domestic economic reforms depends upon obtaining a vastly increased flow of high-technology Western imports, securing freer access to Western markets for Eastern European exports, and opening East European economies to the competition and stimuli of the capitalist world economy.

Since 1989, the nations of Eastern Europe have taken several steps to expand their trade relations with the West, preeminent among which have been the negotiation of trade and economic cooperation agreements with the European Community that will lower tariffs and eliminate quotas for many categories of exports to the EC. Several East European nations even hope to gain EC membership once domestic reforms have created the basic institutions of an open, market-oriented economy.

The question of East European membership is a weighty and controversial one for the EC, especially in light of the ongoing debate on political unification within the European Community. If the EC decides to move rapidly toward political union, including a common foreign and defense policy, then East European membership would be inconceivable without a total transformation in Eastern Europe's external security arrangements. Although several East European nations seem ready to accept the reduction in national sovereignty and the realignment in security relations that EC membership would entail, many West European nations have considerable political and economic reservations about accepting East European applicants in the near future. The task of coordinating economic policy among 12 advanced industrial nations will already be sufficiently complex without the additional complication of incorporating backward and inefficient Eastern European economies into the system. Furthermore, the intra-EC conflicts about achieving political union are already sufficiently contentious without the added factor of potential Eastern European inclusion. So with the partial exception of West Germany and Great Britain, most Western European nations wish to concentrate on the task of unifying the 12-member EC before addressing the issue of East European integration.

Of course, East European membership in the EC cannot be considered seriously until after the East European countries convert their domestic economic systems and external economic relations to a market-oriented basis, a process that will involve among other things the achievement of currency convertibility. The EC is considering the creation and financing of an East European Payments Union to achieve currency convertibility within the CMEA, seeing this as a necessary stage in the transition to full convertibility. But several East European nations regard this proposal as a Western plot to reinforce their ties to the CMEA and deflect their requests for EC membership. A noticeable increase in EC-East European tension seems inevitable as East European desires for membership outpace both economic practicality and EC receptivity.

While the possibility of East European integration into the EC raises a complex set of issues that will take many years to resolve, several other more immediate concerns must also be confronted to strengthen trade relations between Eastern Europe and the West. Most important, the cumbersome array of tariffs, quotas, and restrictions that have historically impeded East European access to Western import supplies and export markets must be streamlined if not eliminated. So far, the nations of the European Community have proven more willing to reduce trade restrictions than the United States, a disparity that reflects a long-standing conflict between the United States and its allies about the fundamental nature and purpose of East bloc trade. Although the United States has historically cultivated only limited economic relations with Eastern Europe and has viewed those relations as a subordinate element of the strategic relationship with the Soviet Union, the West Europeans have developed much stronger commercial linkages with the East European nations and have valued those linkages for their purely economic benefits independent of any strategic considerations.

Nothing illustrates the U.S.-West European conflict about trade with Eastern Europe more clearly than the recent developments within CoCom, the 17-member organization devoted to restricting high technology, strategically sensitive exports to the Eastern bloc. Throughout the 1980s, the West Europeans supported the loosening of CoCom controls on the grounds that many of the restricted items were readily available from other sources and posed no security threat to the West in any event. Then, in 1989, the acceleration of reform within the Eastern bloc intensified West European pressure for restructuring CoCom; most West European governments became convinced that there was no need to maintain an elaborate set of trade restrictions after the military threat that justified their imposition had disappeared. They wished to replace the onerous CoCom controls with a liberal trade environment in which both Western commercial interests and Eastern reform experiments could flourish. But the U.S. government opposed radical reform, fearing that exports to Eastern Europe would be siphoned off to strengthen the Soviet military machine.

It was not until mid-1990 that the United States acknowledged that its stance on CoCom was damaging American commercial interests and costing U.S. firms at least $7 billion in annual exports, while also endangering the progress of East European reforms. As leaders from both Eastern and Western Europe pointed out, U.S. insistence upon export controls deprived East European nations of the communications and industrial technology needed to modernize their productive capacities, develop their financial service systems, and ensure the free flow of information critical to functioning democracy. Under pressure from its own private sector and from its

European allies, the U.S. government agreed in June 1990 to relax CoCom controls on exports of high-technology goods to the Eastern Bloc, particularly to the favored nations of Hungary, Poland, and Czechoslovakia. Although this U.S. concession does not amount to a complete renunciation of the burdensome and increasingly outdated CoCom licensing system, it does represent an important step.

Perhaps the most effective mechanisms for promoting economic regeneration in Eastern Europe are those that contribute directly to the strengthening of market forces within East European economies. A prime example of such mechanisms are investment projects in which Western firms buy out state enterprises or form joint ventures with East European private entrepreneurs. Such investment projects can provide the managerial expertise, advanced technology, and capital to help Eastern Europe manage the transition from inefficient, state-run economies to competitive, market-oriented systems.

The potential advantages for Western investors in Eastern Europe are well known: low labor costs, major new markets, and relatively lax safety and environmental standards. But the drawbacks of investment in Eastern Europe are even more apparent: disastrously low levels of labor and capital productivity, outmoded production facilities, underdeveloped communications and transportation infrastructure, muddled and ambiguous property ownership laws, and extraordinarily cumbersome and irrational taxation and profit repatriation regulations.

When these entrenched problems are placed in the context of the severe recessions currently plaguing most East European economies, it is not surprising that many Western firms are wary about the short-term prospects for profitable investment. Furthermore, Western governments can do only so much to encourage a flow of investment resources to Eastern Europe, through providing insurance and loan guarantees for investment projects. No matter what alluring incentives Western governments dangle before the eyes of potential investors, they cannot force private corporations to provide the investment and expertise critical to Eastern European economic recovery. Only if Western corporations deem East European projects financially sound will they be willing to invest.

Of course, the prospects for Western investment, like the potential for all other types of Western assistance, differ markedly from country to country. East Germany is assured what some see as a glorious future of economic colonization by West Germany—a process that will entail severe short-term unemployment and economic dislocations, but that will ultimately recreate the German economic miracle east of the Elbe. Hungary, Poland, and Czechoslovakia can anticipate a less overwhelming, but still sizable, invasion of Western capital.[9] All three countries are assiduously courting Western investors by revising their tax, investment, and profit repatriation regulations; expanding the scope of the private sector; establishing realistic prices and interest rates; and moving toward currency convertibility. These changes should provide an inviting climate for Western investors with an eye for long-term profit opportunities. By contrast, these countries are laggards in the area of attracting Western investment. With their meager, impoverished domestic markets, their history of discouraging foreign investment, and their reluctance to undertake fundamental domestic economic reforms, Bulgaria and Romania stand little chance of exciting the enthusiasm of Western investors in the near future.

The central issue of Western economic support for Eastern Europe does not involve how much aid to provide, but rather to whom and in what sequence aid should be extended. So far, the Western nations have supplied substantial assistance only to the unequivocally reform-oriented regimes of Hungary and Poland; they have decided to delay the financial rescue and economic integration of Eastern Europe into the West until after the East European countries make

---

9. In fact, both Hungary and Poland have set the ambitious goal of placing one-third of their industrial sectors in the hands of foreign investors by the year 2000.

considerable progress toward consolidating capitalist democracy. This Western strategy of calculated restraint would be most commendable in a private business corporation weighing the costs and benefits of investment in Eastern Europe. But one difference between governments and businesses is that governments can pursue policy objectives that do not generate immediate economic returns and that businesses might eschew as too risky. Certainly, there are risks involved in supporting untested East European reform initiatives. But if the Western nations adopt a wait-and-see attitude, their assistance might come too late. The countries of Eastern Europe are currently undergoing the most difficult and hazardous phase in their transition to democracy, as they confront severe recessions, massive economic dislocations, and intensifying social hardships. It cannot be denied that the people of Eastern Europe must surmount these multiple crises through their own efforts and that Western assistance can only succeed in the context of determined domestic reforms. Yet, it is also undeniable that the critical juncture in Eastern European history has been reached and that the need for Western support is urgent.

IX

The Western nations' exultation about Eastern Europe's escape from Soviet domination is clearly mixed with trepidation concerning the new responsibilities that this geopolitical revolution has thrust upon them. Western countries have reacted to the costs and complications of integrating Eastern Europe economically into the West with some discomfiture. And the looming necessity of integrating Eastern Europe into a larger security framework is occasioning even greater unease in Western capitals. As the states of Eastern Europe sunder their ties to the moribund WTO and drift out of the Soviet orbit, the Western allies will be confronted with the troublesome task of anchoring them in a new European security order. Essentially, the Warsaw Pact has died in

NATO's backyard, and the Western nations must find some discreet way to dispose of the corpse.

The nations of the Western alliance have already agreed that NATO's function must be transformed. Now that the Eastern bloc is no longer perceived as an imminent military threat, everyone concurs with Secretary of State James Baker's handy dictum that NATO's mission must change from preventing war to building peace. However, consensus has not yet been reached on the seemingly obvious corollary that NATO's structure must change along with its function. With the end of the East-West confrontation that generated and sustained the dual alliance system, the rationale for the division of Europe into two separate and antagonistic blocs has lost force. Yet the members of NATO have not formulated a clear vision of how to restructure the relationship between the two blocs. The Soviets and some Western countries have suggested the assimilation of NATO and the WTO into a single common security system such as the CSCE; others have put forward the idea of integrating the East European countries into NATO; while yet others have advocated retaining the original NATO membership intact while letting the Warsaw Pact disintegrate on its own.

The United States has been most resistant to fundamental change in NATO's structure, in part because it is the United States that has the most to lose from the dissolution of the NATO alliance into a pan-European security order. In the view of many U.S. officials, NATO's basic structure should not be tampered with because it provides a stable and reliable geopolitical framework that has preserved peace in Europe throughout the postwar period. Yet, many observers in both Eastern and Western Europe feel that the objectives that have traditionally justified NATO's existence—maintaining stability in Europe, preventing the eruption of territorial conflicts between and within states, verifying arms control agreements on conventional forces—could more effectively be achieved within a pan-European security structure than in a structure that perpetuates the division of Europe.

Although U.S. officials maintain that admitting the East European nations into NATO or assimilating NATO into the CSCE would seriously undermine the cohesiveness, decision-making capacity, and effectiveness of the Western security system, several West European nations, particularly the Germans, contend that incorporation and unification must replace cohesiveness and exclusion as the organizational imperatives of the alliance. A crucial problem, however, is that the Western Europeans have yet to agree even among themselves on a new framework for European security. Fundamental uncertainty persists on issues such as the continued need for NATO to counterbalance resurgent German power in Europe, the prospects for the EC to assume responsibilities in the security realm, and the future role of the CSCE as a bridge between East and West. Thus, although the Europeans are more inclined than the Americans to go beyond tinkering with existing structures to devise a dramatically different foundation for European security, real movement in this direction must await a political and conceptual revolution in the West that is as profound as the changes that have taken place in the East.

In the next few years, pressure from Western Europe and desire to resolve the remaining security questions surrounding the issue of German reunification will likely lead the United States to accept the need for a transformation in the structure as well as the functions of the Western alliance. In the long term, this will entail dispensing with the notion of Western as opposed to European security and building a new military framework to parallel and reinforce the reality of the political and economic integration of Europe. The United States will not play a leading role in this process, but it can at least play a constructive one.

X

Any realistic survey of the future of Eastern Europe must conclude on a sober and cautious note. The region has entered a phase of wrenching change, and the prospects for political stabilization and economic recovery are uncertain. Furthermore, although the West's stake in the future of Eastern Europe is high, its capacity to influence outcomes is limited. Not all East European countries are eager to accept Western tutelage in the implementation of political and economic reforms and the countries that are most receptive to Western advice—Hungary and Poland—are also the countries whose economies are in the state of deepest crisis.

In fact, the West and the Soviet Union share a similar set of constraints and opportunities as they confront the dilemmas of change in Eastern Europe. On the one hand, neither Moscow's troops nor Washington's dollars can ensure stability in Eastern Europe. The solutions to Eastern Europe's problems must come from within, through internal political and economic regeneration. Yet, the USSR and the Western countries do share an opportunity to encourage East European regeneration through cooperative efforts to create a more conducive external environment. If they can agree on a framework to replace military confrontation with political and economic cooperation as the basis of East-West interactions, they will give East European societies the maneuvering room and the resources they need to build more viable economic and political systems.

III

Mixed Blessing: The End of the Cold War in the Third World

Ilya Prizel

A CHAPTER ON THE THIRD WORLD in a book devoted to examining the consequences of change in Europe requires little explanation. Although the Cold War began in and over Europe in the wake of World War II, the Third World turned out to be the main arena of superpower competition during the postwar era. It was conflict in the Third World that brought the United States and the Soviet Union closest to direct military confrontation—over Cuba in 1962 and the Middle East in 1973. And although the division of Europe attained a static equilibrium as early as 1949, with the status of West Berlin remaining as the sole point of contention, it was in the Third World that both superpowers attempted to reshape the international order.

To the extent that the decline of the Soviet-American Cold War conflict in Europe leads to a similar détente in the Third World, an important source of crisis and danger not only for the superpowers, but also for the world as a whole, may be attenuated. Yet, for many Third World nations, the consequences of these developments cannot be wholly welcome. As it was in the nineteenth century, the competition of the world's great powers since 1945 has been for most developing countries the essential key for gaining access to Western financial and technological resources. One result of the decline of U.S.-Soviet competition in the Third World may be to accentuate the already marked disparities between the majority of developing countries and the industrialized world. Another may be to further exacerbate the alienation between North and South and thus contribute to a deepening anomie among the largest part of the world's population. This conclusion follows naturally from a realistic appraisal of the motives and interests that have guided the developed world's policies toward the Third World during the past four decades.

II

The roots of Soviet interest in the developing world can be traced to the beginnings of the Soviet state. Very soon after the foundation of the Soviet Union, its Communist leadership came to view the colonial order as the linchpin of the existing world order. In his classic essay, "Imperialism the Highest Stage of Capitalism," Lenin asserted that the capitalist system could not survive without the exploitation of the colonial world. And because the capitalist world system had now been fully internationalized, he argued, destruction of the colonial system must precede world revolution. Indeed, the destruction of colonialism was deemed far more important than the installation of socialism in the colonial world. Thus, as early as 1919, Lenin's policy was to provide support to any nationalist movement that was anticolonial.

This early Soviet "internationalism" reflected much more than simple opportunism. Despite the hardships imposed on Russia by the civil war, Lenin was willing to extend assistance to nationalist movements throughout Asia, the Levant, and as far away as Latin America. In some instances, this help was enough to create real problems. Russia's intrusion into the colonial societies on its Asian periphery, for example, was seen as a sufficient threat to the well-being of Great Britain that London made the restoration of relations between the two countries subject to the cessation of Soviet agitation in Asia.

Josef Stalin initially followed Lenin's lead and supported Third World nationalists and encouraged alliances between Communists and nationalists. But he abandoned this policy after the 1927 massacre of Chinese Communists by Chiang Kaishek and shunned commitments in the Third World for the rest of his life. On the eve of, and of course during, World War II, he had little interest in alienating the colonial powers whose support he sought in the struggle against fascism. After World War II, when the Soviet Union had become the prime power in the Eastern hemisphere, Stalin became preoccupied with the consolidation of Soviet rule in Eastern Europe. Always distrustful of allies not under his direct control, he refused to support wars of national liberation in the Third World even when led by Communists, as was the case in Greece.[1]

Throughout the post–World War II period, there was a reflexive symmetry in the attitude of the superpowers toward the Third World. In the beginning, neither power expressed much interest in the Third World. Stalin's policy during the early phases of the Cold War was almost entirely Eurocentric, as was the foreign policy of the United States. Aside from pressing Britain to decolonize, U.S. officials paid relatively scant attention to the Third World. Although it was the crisis brought on by the civil war in Greece and Stalin's threat to Turkey that served as a catalyst in the formulation of the Truman Doctrine, George Kennan's 1947 "X" article in *Foreign Affairs*, "The Sources of Soviet Conduct," which provided the first coherent statement of what would soon become the foundation of U.S. foreign policy, almost totally ignored the developing world.

The symmetry in the superpowers' attitude toward the Third World continued into the 1950s, when the outbreak of war on the Korean Peninsula extended the Cold War to Asia and the Middle East, and the success of decolonization after World War II widened the potential area of U.S.-Soviet competition. Stalin, who initially regarded the leaders of the newly independent countries as native agents of the colonial powers, reappraised this attitude and initiated modest diplomatic efforts to establish a Soviet presence throughout Asia. But it was only after Nikita Khrushchev's rise to power that support for wars of "national liberation" became a focal point of a more

---

1. Stalin's only direct involvements in the Third Word were to delay Russia's withdrawal of troops from Iran in 1946 and to extend diplomatic and military support to Israel during its quest for independence.

aggressive Soviet policy toward the Third World. With the incorporation of West Germany into NATO in 1955 and the consolidation of U.S. leadership in Western Europe, the Kremlin had little choice but to shift the arena of its competition with the West to the emerging Afro-Asian bloc. Khrushchev revived the old Leninist concept of collaboration between Communists and nationalists, urging local Communist parties to support independent movements such as Jawaharlal Nehru's Congress Party in India. In addition, Khrushchev launched the notion of "zones of peace," encouraging Asian states on the periphery of the Soviet Union to ascribe to "positive neutralism," which was to entail avoidance of military alliances with the West, curtailment of the role of foreign capital, and development of the public sector as the key to national development.

After the USSR began to extend massive loans to construct large infrastructure and industrial projects, the Eisenhower administration responded in kind. Throughout the late 1940s, Washington's support for decolonization throughout Asia had little evident cost. By the early 1950s, however, U.S. officials—fearing alliances between Communists and nationalists and the emergence of left-leaning neutralism—began to perceive the real price of decolonization as the United States became the prime paymaster of France's effort to retain its colonial presence in Indochina. At the same time, U.S. policy attempted to coopt nationalist Third World leaders with increased U.S. aid. To thwart Soviet-inspired neutralism, Secretary of State John Foster Dulles undertook a crusade to conclude as many military alliances with Third World countries as possible. Dulles also made strenuous (and largely successful) efforts to purge every visible trace of communism or Soviet presence in the Third World. By the early 1950s, responding to U.S. pressures, almost every Latin America state had severed diplomatic ties with the USSR and expelled Communists who served in coalition governments. In Iran and Guatemala, where the local regimes appeared to be too recalcitrant for U.S. preferences, the Eisenhower administration engineered military coups to oust the errant regimes.

This overt American shift to supporting colonial regimes in the Third World, which was backed up with not very covert American intervention, presented the USSR with an opportunity to become an arms supplier to radical Third World regimes and less directly to various liberation movements. Thus, from 1955 (the year the first "Czech"-Egyptian weapons deal was signed) the USSR, in addition to supplying a host of radical Third World regimes with military and economic aid, established contacts with liberation movements such as Kenya's Mao-Mao and Algeria's National Liberation Front (FLN).

Responding to a perception of growing Soviet success throughout the Third World, the administration of President John F. Kennedy decided to bolster the U.S. position there through seemingly contradictory means. On the one hand, Kennedy decided that the United States should be on the "right side of change" and encourage the development of democratic institutions throughout the Third World, backing that process with substantial transfers of resources through newly created or revived agencies such as the Alliance for Progress, Food for Peace, the Peace Corps, and so forth. The second, and seemingly contradictory, component of Kennedy's policy was the effort to enhance the United States' ability to project force into the Third World. It was during the Kennedy period that the United States adopted the doctrine of limited war and began to invest heavily in the development of "counter-insurgency" capabilities. This policy was designed not only to enhance the United States' own ability to project force into the Third World, but also—through sale of U.S. weapons and training—to reinforce the capabilities of indigenous armed forces to meet the "Communist challenge." The steady extension of the American commitment to and involvement in Vietnam was but one outgrowth of Kennedy's vaunted declaration to "bear any burden," "pay any price" in defense of freedom.

In hindsight, the 1960s appear as the years of greatest superpower enthusiasm, as both sides competed energetically to validate their respective philosophies of history. By the end of the decade, however, the Third World policies of both the United States and the USSR were in disarray. The war in Vietnam not only shattered U.S. confidence in its ability to control events in the Third World, but it also destroyed the foreign policy consensus of its political elite at home. The USSR did not experience a disaster akin to Vietnam, yet it too suffered a string of bitter disappointments in the Third World. Several charismatic Third World leaders on whom Moscow had spent lavishly were discredited, most notoriously Egypt's Gamal Abdal Nasser following the 1967 war with Israel. Others, including Indonesia's Sukarno, Algeria's Ben Bella, and Ghana's Kwame Nkrumah were ousted from office altogether. Furthermore, despite massive Soviet aid to the Third World's public sector, none of the recipients of Soviet aid—other than Cuba and South Yemen—appeared to be moving toward building socialism. Many Soviet-sponsored economic projects that were intended to demonstrate the relevance of the Soviet model to the Third World turned out to be "white elephants" that only drained the resources of both the USSR and the recipient country. The High Dam at Aswan is the most visible, but scarcely isolated, example of a Soviet-built project that went wrong.

III

Détente was launched during this period, at a time when the Soviet Union was about to attain nuclear parity, and both superpowers had become wary of the Third World. Although it is beyond the scope of this paper to deal with each party's broader interest in détente, it is important to note that the role of the Third World in the international order was a key component. Signed during the 1972 Moscow summit, the Basic Principles Agreement (BPA) committed each side to consult the other when faced with an imminent crisis that might force the parties into a potentially volatile situation. In fact, although there are numerous explanations for the collapse of détente in the 1970s, including strong domestic reactions in the Soviet

Union as well as the United States, it is clear that conflict over Third World issues played a central role in the demise of the superpowers' effort to redefine their relationship in the 1970s.

In retrospect, it appears that U.S. leaders expected that the rewards of détente would reduce the incentives for Soviet adventurism in the Third World and enable Washington to continue with the devolution of global responsibility announced in the Nixon Doctrine. The Soviet interpretation of détente was quite different. From Brezhnev down, the Soviet leadership asserted that détente had denied Washington the pretext of Soviet threat as a justification for launching new interventions in the Third World.[2] Russian leaders declared that the Soviet Union had a moral obligation to help the Third World attain "liberation," an obligation that Brezhnev enshrined in the 1977 Soviet constitution.

The conflict emerging from this clash of interpretations of détente was further aggravated by the superpowers' very different responses to their particular experiences in the Third World. Reeling from its Vietnam experience, the United States was in the midst of an unhappy retreat from its assertive position in the Third World, a retreat made all the more difficult to manage as it was imposed in part by legislation that sharply curtailed the power of the executive branch and in part through substantial cuts in its defense allocations. In response to its previous disappointments, the Soviet Union decided in the future to bolster its position in the Third World by supporting those radical regimes that were led by a "vanguard party," rather than a charismatic leader and to enhance the survivability of these regimes by expanding the Soviet capacity to project force deep into the Third World. Given the very different interpretations of détente and the very different expectations

---

2. For an elaboration of Soviet analysis of the impact of détente on the Third World, see the author's *Latin America through Soviet Eyes: The Evolution of Soviet Perceptions of Latin America during the Brezhnev Years, 1964-1982* (Cambridge: Cambridge University Press, 1990), 27–30.

each superpower harbored, it was only a matter of time before the two states would collide in the Third World.

Indeed, it was a sequence of events in the Third World that provided the most immediate occasion for the demise of détente. The failure of the USSR to apprise the United States about the impending Arab-Israeli War in 1973 was the first incident to raise questions in the United States about the willingness of the USSR to forgo gain in the Third World for the sake of a more stable international system. After the expansion of Soviet-Cuban involvement in Angola in 1975, President Gerald Ford was forced to drop the term détente from his 1976 presidential campaign, and the Soviet invasion of Afghanistan in December 1979 forced President Jimmy Carter to scuttle the SALT II treaty and impose economic sanctions on the USSR. Soviet-Cuban aid to Nicaragua and Nicaragua's aid to the FMLN in El Salvador further convinced many in Washington that Russia intended to persist with expansionary policies, even if those policies directly challenged U.S. national interests.

The shock of the relentless Russian expansion played a significant role in the failure of President Carter's reelection bid and brought an end to America's Vietnam-induced weariness in the international arena. The election of Ronald Reagan to the presidency in 1980 signaled a new departure for U.S. policy toward the Third World. Unlike the Carter administration—which saw Third World conflicts primarily in their North-South or strictly regional context—the Reagan administration viewed upheaval in the Third World almost exclusively through the lens of East-West relations and was determined to contain perceived Soviet expansion. Among the most salient changes in the U.S. policy introduced by the Reagan administration were the decisions to drop Carter's emphasis on human rights and, instead, lend support to any Third World regime that might be helpful to the United States in containing the Soviet Union. Thus, countries with tainted human rights records such as Pakistan, South Africa, Zaire, Argentina, and El Salvador were embraced by the Reagan administration as allies in the struggles against Soviet-supported movements or governments. Although the Reagan administration was not able to overcome U.S. public opposition to the introduction of U.S. forces in Third World conflicts, it was able to garner congressional support to supply insurgents with sufficient military and economic aid to debilitate these regimes in Afghanistan, Angola, Kampuchea, and Nicaragua to a point at which they could not impose a military solution or arrest the economic deterioration they were experiencing.

The initial response of the Soviet Union to the Reagan administration's new assertiveness was muted; Soviet leaders Andropov and Chernenko were apparently too frail, their holds on power too tenuous to enable them to formulate a coherent response to the U.S. challenge. With Mikhail Gorbachev's rise to power in 1985, however, Soviet policy quickly regained its assertiveness as the Soviet leadership moved aggressively to protect the interests of its clients. During his first year in office, Gorbachev substantially increased both the quality and quantity of weapons furnished by the USSR to Nicaragua, Afghanistan, and Angola. In the case of Afghanistan, the Soviet armed forces went on the offensive, for the first time resorting to heavy aerial bombardment of the *Mujahidin* and to air raids on refugee camps in Pakistan.

Yet, this escalation by the Soviet Union also enabled the Reagan administration to overcome congressional opposition to providing the Afghan guerrillas with Stinger shoulder-fired surface-to-air missiles and won support for millions of dollars in aid to Angola's anti-Marxist UNITA and Nicaragua's Contras. The influx of U.S. aid rapidly altered the situation on the battlefield. In Afghanistan, the Soviet armed forces started to suffer larger and, as it turned out, unacceptable losses, rapidly eroding what was left of Soviet public support for the intervention. In Angola and Nicaragua, although the Soviet help succeeded in assuring that U.S.-backed insurgents would not be able to topple the regime militarily, it soon became clear that no amount of Soviet aid and no number of Cuban troops would be sufficient to suppress the insurgents to a point where they would cease to sap the vitality of these countries' economies. Thus, although military victory had become elusive, the economic costs of adhering to a largely military strategy became more and more painfully clear.

The success of Reagan's policy came at a particularly difficult moment in Soviet history. By the early 1970s, the Soviet economy (whose growth had begun to lose momentum at the end of the 1960s) slipped into total stagnation, if not negative growth. Brezhnev managed to shield the economic deterioration of the country from the Soviet public mainly by starving the Soviet industrial plants from new investment and increasing some imports, financed through sales of gold and oil. By the mid-1980s, however, years of neglect of the Soviet infrastructure had started to manifest themselves with an accelerating decline in Soviet productivity. Aggravating this phenomenon, the very high prices of oil and gold—which enabled the Kremlin during the 1970s to preserve a semblance of health in the Soviet economy—had sharply declined, fetching prices in 1987 no higher in real terms than in 1974. Today, the USSR, after a decade of almost negative economic growth, faces huge internal and current account deficits, collapsing productivity, ever-more critical food shortages, and increasing ethnic tensions exacerbated by economic hardship. There has even been open discussion at the highest levels of Soviet government about the likelihood of an economic collapse. Given the dire state of the Soviet economy, the Kremlin appears to be far more eager to acquire the best possible credit and technology transfer arrangements from the Western powers than to attempt to alter the global "correlation of forces" by supporting radical regimes in the Third World.

Abroad, the experiences of Afghanistan, Angola, Nicaragua, and indirectly Cambodia, have finally impressed upon Moscow that it does not have a monopoly on supporting successful insurgencies in the Third World. The Reagan administration's willingness to provide substantial economic and military aid to anti-Marxist insurgents have turned the Soviet Third World victories of the 1970s into bleeding wounds that further weaken

Russia's anemic economy. Increasingly, Soviet analysts note that Russia's adventures in the Third World accomplished for the USSR little more than the impoverishment of the Soviet treasury, the creation of unnecessary tensions with the West and China, and the creation of a string of client regimes that appear to have no prospect of surviving without Soviet aid.

IV

Soviet domestic difficulties and profound disappointment with the Soviet experience in developing countries have lead the USSR to limits its policy instruments in the Third World. The feeble Soviet economy now restrains economic aid from Moscow even to those Third World regimes that profess Marxist orientation, as the cases of Nicaragua and Mozambique illustrate. Gorbachev's decision to reduce Russia's military budget and substantially cut the size of its standing conventional forces will ultimately lead to a decline in the availability of surplus Russian military hardware and thus reduce Moscow's ability to supply potential clients with large quantities of cheap weapons on short notice. Finally, Moscow's decision to cut the size of the Soviet fleet and reduce its global presence will further erode the USSR's ability to project force into areas remote from Russia's periphery. There can be little doubt that the Marxist regimes of Cuba and Nicaragua have been less than reassured by the fact that, since Gorbachev came to power in 1985, the Soviet Navy has not made a single visit to the Caribbean.

Another factor that significantly hampers further Soviet expansion into the Third World is the declining attractiveness of the Soviet model. Unlike the four decades between the 1920s and the 1960s when the Soviet Union served as a cultural and political model to future Third World leaders such as India's Nehru and Turkey's Mustafa Kemal Atatürk, today few in the Third World find the Soviet Union's model very attractive. It is the West that is setting the pace of popular culture throughout the world. Third World elites, even those who profess Marxism, almost universally send their children to be educated in Western countries, particularly in the United States. The Soviet economic model, which a generation of Third World leaders viewed as a prescription for rapid modernization and nation building, turned out to be an economic fiasco. Those Third World countries that have attempted to follow the Soviet model—through the establishment of heavy industry and a large state sector within the economy—discovered that most of the Pharaonic projects became unproductive and unsustainable (often even before their completion), and the state sector encouraged by Moscow turned out to be a massive inefficient behemoth draining precious resources from already feeble economies. It is clear that the only Third World countries that managed to break out of their poverty were those that relied on market mechanisms.

Soviet economic leverage in the Third World has also been severely hampered by the incompatibility of the economy of the USSR with those of most developing countries. Given the state of the Soviet economy, the USSR cannot be a significant source of capital for the Third World; furthermore, given the backwardness of Soviet technology, the limited Soviet credits that are made available to developing countries often go unused. In the main an exporter of primary commodities, the USSR is often a competitor—rather than a market—for the Third World. The unnattractiveness of the Soviet economic model to the Third World was best described by the eminent Chilean economist André Gunder Frank who wrote: "the socialist countries have failed to establish a division of labor and market as a viable alternative to the world capitalist one, either for themselves or even less for ˙non-capitalist development,˙ ˙socialist-oriented˙ progressive Third World countries and liberation movements."[3]

---

3. André Gunder Frank, "The Socialist Countries in the World Economy: The East-South Dimension" in Brigitte Schulz and William Hansen, eds., *The Soviet Bloc and the Third World: The Political Economy of East-South Relations* (Boulder, Colo: Westview Press, 1988), 23.

The economic decline of the USSR has had several profound effects on its foreign policy. Soviet expansion into the Third World—which Brezhnev saw as a manifestation of the viability of Soviet socialism—is now viewed by the Kremlin's new leaders as an expensive luxury that drained Russia of its dwindling resources without providing anything tangible in return. Worse, as the Kremlin's leaders have begun to recognize, Moscow's expansion in the Third World helped to bring about the coalescence of China and the United States and induced America's largest peacetime military buildup. Gorbachev and his team understand that if the Soviet Union is to break the Gordian knot of related social and political anomie that is slowly strangling its economy, Russia will need to reduce its military burden and attract Western capital and technology.

Given the history of the previous decade, few in Moscow believe that a fundamental change in its relations with the West, and particularly with the United States, is possible while the Soviet Union continues to pursue an expansionist policy in the Third World. The reorientation in Moscow's attitude toward the Third World, accordingly, has been swift and profound. As David Albright has observed, by 1987, leading advocates of radical transformation in the Third World—men such as Politburo member Georgi Romanov and head of the International Department of the Communist Party Boris Ponomarev and his deputy Rostislav Ulianovsky—had been replaced by those who favor a broader pattern of economic relations with Third World states, including capitalist ones. Among those who support a less confrontational policy in the Third World are Foreign Minister Eduard Shevardnadze and Politburo members Alexander Yakovlev, Karen Brutents (the new deputy director of the international department), and academician Yevgeni Primakov of the Institute of International Relations and World Economy.[4]

---

4. David E. Albright, "USSR and the Third World in the 1980's," *Problems of Communism*, March-June 1989.

Despite the very serious problems faced by the USSR, it would be wrong to assume that the USSR has totally given up its great power ambitions and thus lost all interest in the Third World. What Gorbachev is attempting to do is bring Soviet commitments closer in line with the ability of Moscow to sustain them. Furthermore, to cure the anemic Soviet economy, Gorbachev is committed to reducing tensions with Russia's principal rival, the United States, seeking simultaneously to reduce Soviet defense outlays and create a more attractive environment for foreign capital and technology. Both aspects of Gorbachev's policy—his desire to preserve influence in the Third World and his desire to do so at less cost—are evident in the series of initiatives he has launched in the Third World. In Afghanistan, for example, after a futile effort to establish a government acceptable to all factions, the USSR withdrew all its troops from the country, thus ending a nine-year effort to defend the Marxist regime it installed in December 1979. Yet, the Soviet Union continues a massive supply effort to the Najibullah regime in Kabul that has enabled it to defy Western expectations and survive in power.

In the case of Nicaragua, the USSR was the first to endorse the Arias Peace Plan, and Nicaragua's Daniel Ortega agreed to hold direct talks with the Contras only after a tense meeting with Gorbachev when the former visited Moscow in November of 1987.[5] However, Soviet pressure on Nicaragua to find a political solution to its problem was again accompanied by ever larger transfers of Russian military materiel. True to Russia's declaratory policy that it will abide by the results of free elections in Nicaragua under the agencies of the Esquipulas II agreement, Moscow cooperated with Washington by exercising its influence on Cuba to halt Cuban shipments of weapons to El Salvador and

---

5. Ilya Prizel, "Latin America: The Long March," *The National Interest*, no. 12 (Summer 1988): 115-117.

pressed the Sandinistas to accept the results of a genuine election.[6]

In Angola, despite undisguised tension with Cuba's Fidel Castro, Moscow resumed contacts with South Africa and used its leverage to bring both Cuba and Angola to terms with UNITA and South Africa. In Southeast Asia, Gorbachev startled the Vietnamese when he offered to withdraw the Soviet fleet from Cam Ranh Bay in exchange for a U.S. pullout from the Philippines and pressed Hanoi to devise a way to withdraw their troops from Cambodia. Similarly, in the case of the Korean Peninsula, Moscow reached out to South Korea by sending its athletes to the Summer Olympics in Seoul and by inviting the key South Korean opposition leader, Kim Young Sam, to meet with North Korean Politburo member Ho Dam.[7] Gorbachev's meeting with South Korean President Roh Tae Woo in San Francisco (after his summit with President George Bush in Washington) was additional illustration of how far Moscow's position has changed since the days when it shunned all contacts with Seoul.

It is clear that the Soviet Union has been was forced by the decadent state of its economy to fundamentally rethink its Third World posture. It is equally clear that the willingness of the Reagan administration to support insurgents opposing Soviet-supported radical regimes and its readiness to commit significant resources to curb the USSR's expansion was a catalyst in shaping Russia's new posture in the Third World.

V

The question that now faces America, Russia, and the Third World is what kind of world order will these players seek to create in the age of "new thinking" in Russia and how will

---

6. See Michael Kramer, "Anger, Bluff and Cooperation," *Time*, June 4, 1990, pp. 38-45.

7. *Washington Post*, June 15, 1989.

they interpret the principles of the flowering second détente? Will the United States, flush with the success of its "rollback" of Soviet power in Eastern Europe and the Third World, experience the same euphoria it felt following the 1962 Cuban missile crisis and attempt to translate its success on a global scale, as it did in the mid-1960s? Will Washington, responding to a more agreeable Soviet Union, revive Franklin D. Roosevelt's idea of "police chiefs" consisting of the permanent members of the United Nations Security Council and thus attempt to arrive at a condominium arrangement with Moscow? Will both superpowers—increasingly preoccupied with their relative economic declines—ignore the Third World and become increasingly inward looking? Or will the new assertiveness of the Third World be such that neither power will be able to exercise significant influence?

Before analyzing the impact of the Third World on the relationship between the superpowers, it is important to note impact of fundamental changes that have taken place elsewhere in the international system. The events that unfolded in Europe during the autumn and winter of 1989 fundamentally weakened the global status of both the United States and the Soviet Union. The reunification of Germany and the accelerated movement toward a united Europe hold forth the prospect of an emerging bloc with a population and GDP considerably larger than that of either superpower. Indeed, the military might of Russia and America, which has enabled them to dominate the international system for nearly 50 years largely proved to be irrelevant during the epoch-making events in the heart of Europe, despite the huge concentration of Soviet and U.S. forces in that part of the world.

Instead of leading the international system, both Russia and America are working hard to preserve what they can of their once dominant voice in Europe. The United States by attempting to breathe life into the ghost of NATO and Russia by trying to circumscribe the sovereignty of a united Germany are waging parallel, and increasingly desperate, battles to avoid being left out of European counsels altogether. Given the return of both superpowers' preoccupation with Europe, it is only obvious that the ability of the Third World to capture the attention of either has significantly diminished.

Perhaps the most important change in the psychology of Russia and America is that both superpowers have now endured very similar traumatic experiences in the Third World. The United States as a result of its debacle in Vietnam and the Soviet Union as a result of its fiasco in Afghanistan have learned the same lesson that Britain acquired from the Boer War (1899-1902)—that there is a limit to the ability of even a great power to reshape the world in its image. Not only did the superpowers acquire an acute sense of the limits of their military might, but in addition the publics of both have become very actively averse to involvements in "local" wars. As a result of their unhappy experiences, it is far less likely that either nation will be willing to undertake the kind of open-ended military commitments in the Third World they had in the past. Thus, direct power projection by the superpowers into the Third World—an event that often brought the superpowers to the verge of confrontation in the past—has largely ceased to be a threat.

Yet, although both superpowers have lost their appetite for direct large-scale intervention in the Third World, and even though both appear to be keen on not allowing the Third World to undermine their improved mutual relationship, the scenario that is least likely to unfold is the emergence of a U.S.-Soviet condominium in the Third World. One key obstacle to any such development is the fact that to agree upon a condominium arrangement in the Third World would require both states to denude their foreign policies of all ideological content—an impossible prospect. It must be remembered that Russia and America each have expended trillions of dollars and built their alliance systems in the name of universal missions; a condominium arrangement between the two superpowers would destabilize their respective alliance systems and distress their domestic political cohesion, a prospect that both states would rather avoid. In fact, it might well be argued that a total de-ideologization of Russian and American foreign policy is not only difficult, but potentially dangerous. For the United States to abandon its universal mission may well auger a return to isolationism, with all its destabilizing effects on the international system. And were Russia to be forced to abandon its international role, the consequence might well be a rise in xenophobic Great-Russian nationalism, intolerance for various ethnic minorities, and a heightened prospect of civil strife in a country that happens to possess the world's largest nuclear arsenal. Indeed, even if we are witnessing the end of the Cold War and a new détente, it is most unlikely that the two super-powers will ever be able to put aside their most basic interests and assume the role of cooperative "police chiefs" envisioned by President Roosevelt after World War II. The inability of the superpowers to cooperate on the settlement of the Afghan war, the Arab-Israeli crisis, and other vital points illustrates the limits of Russo-American collaboration.

VI

Does the apparent decline of Soviet interest in the Third World afford the United States an opportunity to regain a predom-inant global position similar to the one it held in the 1950s? Although such a prospect may indeed be appealing to some in the United States, in reality the potential for such uncontested reengagement is nil. Despite its faltering economy, the USSR could not fully extricate itself from the Third World even if it wanted to. Several key Third World countries, including Algeria, Cuba, Iran, and Turkey, have extensive economic links to the Soviet Union and will continue to draw the USSR into the global arena even if Russia were to attempt to embark on an isolationist course. Even Third World countries that are remote from Russia and have minimal trade with the Soviet Union—countries such as Mexico, Brazil, or Zimbabwe—continue to view Russia's global presence as a guarantee of their political independence and, therefore, will continue to cultivate ties with Moscow despite the precipitous decline in

Russia's global standing. Moreover, although it is true that Russia's military might may well be reduced by Gorbachev's policies, the Soviet Union will remain a military colossus that will continue to cast its long shadow across the Third World. Turkey's recent refusal to allow American technicians to inspect a MiG-29 plane that defected from the USSR is but one indication of Russia's continuing ability to intimidate a Third World country, even a member of NATO.

It is also worth bearing in mind that despite Russia's current economic weakness, with or without successful reform, the Soviet Union may yet become an important economic player in the Third World. As Western Europe moves toward complete economic integration and as long as the resources of what used to be called the Eastern Bloc are absorbed in reconstruction, Europe's markets are likely to become even less open to Third World products. And with Japan busily rebuilding its "co-prosperity" sphere along Asia's Pacific Rim, virtually ignoring all of Africa and Latin America, while the United States confronts its huge current account deficit and implements a free-trade agreement with Canada and weighs making another with Mexico that may reduce the Third World's access to North American markets, the Soviet Union with its willingness to barter—often accepting Third World industrial products in exchange for Russian raw materials—has an opportunity to become an important economic partner (even if not vital) to a large, rapidly growing segment of the Third World.

Neither is it at all evident that Russia's growing weakness in the Third World necessarily translates into growing American strength in that part of the world. In fact, the United States' ability to influence events in the Third World has also been eroding over the last 20 years. On the economic front, America has lost its position as the predominant lender to the Third World. Since the early 1980s, the United States itself was transformed from the world's prime creditor nation to its largest debtor. The American banking system, overexposed in the Third World, narrowly survived the collapse of the Continental Bank of Illinois, which required the largest bailout in American history and is now reeling from the consequences of the far more massive failure of the national savings and loans system. During the long period of rapid global economic expansion that followed the recessions of 1982-1983, Japanese and European banks acquired new international presence, while American banks were forced systematically to reduce their international exposure and, often, fold their global operations. In the next decade, the United States will continue to be bogged down in endless and damaging debt repayment talks with the Third World. Even if old business can be settled satisfactorily, finding new sources of investment and technology transfer is bound to prove difficult.

Indicators of the decline of U.S. financial leadership are many. Currently, the three countries that hold the largest monetary reserves are Taiwan, West Germany, and Japan. A more telling illustration of the decline of the dollar is provided by the case of the Philippines: In that country, which was an American colony and which still retains a special relationship with the United States, Japan has superseded the United States as its largest source of aid, making it only appropriate that the last international meeting analyzing the Filipino economy was held in Tokyo. The relative economic weakness of the United States vis-à-vis the Third World was perhaps best illustrated by the fact that U.S. economic embargoes proved to be ineffective in dislodging regimes even in weak and dependent countries such as Nicaragua and Panama. Nor did U.S. economic pressure on either Libya or Iran have a measurable impact on the policies of these countries.

Even more precipitous has been the decline in America's ability to project force in the Third World. As the war in Vietnam demonstrated, much of America's military might cannot be used effectively in Third World settings. Moreover, unless military involvement is short and relatively bloodless (as was the case in Grenada), it is extremely difficult to sustain public support for any such operation. The ease with which Syria managed to eject the U.S. peacekeeping presence in Lebanon offers a compelling illustration of America's declining ability to control events in the Third World when confronted by a regional power; the unwillingness of the U.S. Congress to fully support President Reagan's policy in Central America provides another.

America's Third World policy has been hampered not only by growing economic and military weakness, but also by the withdrawal of the kind of lukewarm or tacit political support from its allies that once enabled it to act easily in the developing countries. Unlike the United States, which still sees most Third World conflicts in East-West terms, most of America's European allies tend to view these conflicts in their North-South context. In fact, many Europeans see turmoil in the Third World, particularly in Central and South America, as part of a long-term process in which the native populations are attempting to decolonize by expelling U.S. influence in a manner similar to that which occurred in Asia and Africa following World War II. Thus, to most Europeans, America's policy in the Third World represents a futile effort to arrest an inevitable historic process, an adventure for which Europe has little patience or interest. The parochial attitude of America's allies, along with a feeling that they have no responsibility to uphold international order or contain developing country conflict, further isolates America from Europe and Japan when it comes to dealing with the Third World.

The roots of this trend, of course, long predate the present phase of U.S.-Soviet relations. Despite the fact that the Soviet Union had started to resupply Egypt and Syria with military hardware during the 1973 Arab-Israeli War and despite the fact that a nonresponse by the United States would have severely undermined U.S. credibility throughout the world (especially in Europe), no European country other than Portugal was willing to allow the United States to use its airspace to resupply Israel. The parochialism of America's allies and its impact on the Third World are also reflected in the response of Europe and Japan to the Persian Gulf War: Although both Europe and Japan are far more dependent on the free flow of oil through the Straits of Hormuz, neither the Europeans nor the Japanese were willing to take a lead in assuring freedom of navigation at the height of the Iran-Iraq War, choosing to wait for America to act and only then joining in a marginal capacity.

VII

No discussion of the relationship between the superpowers and the Third World can be complete without an analysis of the changes that have taken place in the Third World itself. The defeat of America in Vietnam and of Russia in Afghanistan had an exhilarating impact on the entire Third World. Much as the Russo-Japanese War (1904-1905) showed to the rest of Asia that a "colored" people could defeat a "white" people and thus unleashed a prolonged reaction that ultimately undid the European empires in Asia, the defeat of the superpowers by developing countries has had a bracing impact on the developing countries today. Unlike 20 years ago, few Third World regimes any longer fear that a direct superpower's intervention will dislodge them from power.

During the last 20 years, the superpowers not only lost their ability to threaten Third World regimes with direct intervention, they lost their chief means of indirect intervention—a virtual monopoly on weapon supplies. Until the late 1960s, only the superpowers and a handful of European countries were able to supply military hardware. Today a dozen Third World countries have become eager suppliers of war materiel, ranging from advanced jet aircraft to components essential for chemical and nuclear weapons. The inability of the superpowers to control the flow of arms and military technologies into the Third World has further weakened the role of the superpowers in Third World affairs.

The political, military, and economic weakness of the superpowers vis-à-vis the Third World has been further accentuated by the almost universal disillusionment of the Third World with economic and social models from the developed world. The rise of Islamic fundamentalism as a challenge to the pro-capitalist Shah of Iran and to the socialist government of

Algeria and the rise of *Sendero Luminoso* and the *Tupac Amaru* group in Peru are but the most extreme examples of a broad trend toward the rejection of all foreign models—socialist as well as capitalist—in favor of indigenous political ideologies. The declining appeal of all manners of Western ideology is itself the expression of a growing xenophobia in large parts of the Third World that has undercut the authority and often the access of the superpowers in the Third World.

The decline of the superpowers' ability to influence events in the Third World is, in some respects, both a symptom of, and a form of compensation for, the decline of the importance of much of the Third World in the international system. In economic terms, the Third World's share in global trade has fallen almost every year since the Korean War. The explosive growth in world trade that took place after that war occurred overwhelmingly within countries of the OECD and the Pacific Rim. With the exception of nations such as Mexico and India, which constitute major trading partners of the United States and the USSR respectively, few Third World countries have emerged as significant world economic players. Instead, the basic trend has been one of relative decline from an inferior position in the world economy. Even the historic dependence of the developed world on the mineral wealth of the Third World has sharply declined. In the case of Russia, its own mineral wealth is so diverse that it has no need for the minerals of the Third World. In the case of the West, the decline in the utilization of minerals per unit of production along with the ever-growing availability of synthetic substitutes has led to an ever-diminishing need for Third World minerals. Thus, unlike the 1950s and 1960s—when both superpowers jealously watched each other expand in the Third World, fearing that such expansion might directly undercut their respective economies—in the late 1980s, neither of the superpowers sees most of the Third World as vital to their economic well-being.

Another factor that has diminished the Third World's importance to the superpowers is the acceleration of technological breakthroughs in strategic weapons, which have made physical presence near the periphery of one's opponent a far less decisive military factor. Unlike the 1950s when the Eisenhower administration attempted to ring the USSR with an almost con-tinuous string of American military bases from Norway to Korea, and unlike the early 1960s when Khrushchev tried to break out of that encirclement by placing medium-range ballistic missiles in Cuba, by the 1980s, most considerations of geographic access had become void. In an era of submarine-launched ballistic missiles, sea-based cruise missiles, and highly accurate multiple-warhead ballistic missiles, physical presence along the periphery of one's potential foe serves little practical purpose other than facilitating some secondary electronic eavesdropping. Thus, the era when the USSR was willing to put up millions of rubles to gain landing rights in such "key" strategic points as Conakry Guinea, or the United States to spend millions of dollars for a "vital asset" such as Diego Garcia is essentially over.

IX

If the superpowers are far less able to control events in the Third World, and indeed have fewer vital interests there than they did in the past, what does this imply for the future evolution of the international system? Although the historic analogies are always dangerous to apply, it appears that present circumstances parallel the world situation that existed before the great imperial rush of 1882. In the center, the inter-national system has begun to move away from the bipolar world that dominated it since 1945 and, instead, a group of five unequal poles of power have started to emerge—the United States, the Soviet Union, Europe, China, and Japan. The Third World, too, has begun to fragment, along three separate lines. The first line of cleavage separates countries with dynamic economies located along the Pacific Rim and South Asia; these countries have the potential to become vital pillars of the emerging world order (in fact it is already a misnomer to refer to these countries as "Third World" countries). Another group of countries, which includes Mexico, Brazil, India, Iran, and Saudi Arabia may, despite their continued backwardness, by virtue of location or mineral base, continue to receive the attention of at least some, if not all, of the great powers.

Finally, the fate of the great majority of the Third World will most likely be to become increasingly marginalized in the international system, falling ever further behind the rest of the world. One predictable result of this isolation will be to fuel chaos and turmoil in some parts of the developing world. Another will be to encourage the already apparent tendency among domestic elites to grope for alternative, non-Western forms of sociocultural and economic organization. How destructive these experiments might be can be judged from their results in Iran and Peru, and perhaps also Kampuchea. It has been argued that the survival of some radical Marxist regimes in the Third World should be seen more a manifestation of the Third World's frustration with its marginalization within the international system, rather than a clairvoyant attempt by Moscow to shift the arena of competition with America from the center of the periphery.[8] Viewed in light of the worst excesses resulting from the Third World's social unrest, the seemingly anachronistic survival of loyalty to socialist ideals in some Third World states should be welcomed, perhaps even encouraged, as the sole surviving vestige of Western influence.

---

8. Charles H. Fairbanks, "Gorbachev's Global Doughnut: The Empire with a Hole in the Middle," *The National Interest*, no. 19 (Spring 1990).

PART TWO

Old Realities:
Continuities of Statecraft

IV

The "Revisionists": Germany and Russia in a Post-Bipolar World

Josef Joffe

ONLY THREE NATIONS always have been able to change the postwar order in Europe: the United States, the Soviet Union, and Germany. Of the three, the United States has been the holder of the balance, thus in essence the power of the status quo. The duo in search of change have been Germany and Russia, and it is no accident that these are also the two players around or against whom the postwar system was constructed.

That the two superpowers could undo the status quo need not be labored. The United States and the Soviet Union built and maintained the postwar system as by-product of their global rivalry, which was centered, above all, on Europe. Whence it follows that either of them could have changed that order unilaterally—merely by withdrawing from it. Whoever abandoned the contest of containment and countercontainment, would transform a European strategic landscape that, for almost half a century after World War II, was defined by balance, bipolarity, and stalemate. In the absence of the United States, a nuclear-armed Soviet Union would gain a position of strategic primacy on the Continent. Similarly, the retraction of Soviet power, beginning in the fall of 1989, has already changed the status quo. Its empire in Eastern Europe collapsed very quickly thereafter, and, as a result, America's raison d'être on the Continent might collapse as well.

But why Germany, why not France or Britain? The reason hinges more on geography than on nuclear weapons or (formal) great power status, which only the British and French possess. The postwar order was built in and around Germany, with the two successors of the Third Reich, the Federal Republic (FRG) and the German Democratic Republic (GDR), assuming critical roles in the system's maintenance. Situated at the fulcrum of the European balance, each Germany became the strategic brace of its alliance. It is in Germany where the two countervailing coalitions have met; it is Germany that hosted the largest peacetime concentration of power the Continent has ever seen.

Now assume that united Germany were to leave NATO. France virtually did so in 1966 when de Gaulle expelled American forces from French soil, while withdrawing from the integrated command structure. That, however, had as little effect on the overall balance as did Spain's accession to NATO in 1981; indeed, there are few who even remember these two dates. By contrast, a momentous shift in the balance of military and political power would ensue if Germany became neutral. Disalignment would trigger profound realignment, and whatever the actual consequences might be, they would undo whatever were left of the postwar order after the completion of the Soviet Union's withdrawal.

NATO, or what remained of it, would be bottled up behind the Rhine, stripped of depth and its most important military asset on the Continent. The United States would be thrown back on a rump alliance centered on Britain, perhaps on France, too. The bulk of U.S. troops in Europe (213,000) has been stationed in West Germany; where would they or, more precisely, their remnant find another home? Whether NATO's Northern Flank (Denmark, Norway) or the Southern Flank (Greece, Turkey) would remain in the alliance as isolated islands is an open question. Central Europe, in any case, would once more be a distinct geographic entity—beholden to German influence if the Soviet Union could exact German neutrality as a price for complete withdrawal behind the Bug River.

The permutations of this game may be endless, but there is no gainsaying the basic fact: Among the medium powers, the player of maximum impact is Germany because of what it has and where it is. By dint of its economic potential, Germany represents, apart from the two superpowers, the most critical weight in the European balance, and it also occupies the decisive strategic space in it—at the very center.

II

Why should Germany (or before 1990, the FRG) and Russia be in the vanguard of system change? In a basic sense, these two nations always have been the two "revisionist" actors on the postwar stage.[1] The remaining lead players, the United States, Britain, and France, have been the status quo powers. Double-containment was their basic purpose: Explicitly, their post-Hitler alliance was directed against the Soviet Union, the most recent contender to hegemony in Europe; implicitly, the coalition was directed against the previous claimant, Germany. Indeed, the five-member Western Union, joining Britain, France, and the Benelux countries, formally targeted Germany as source of the threat as late as March 17, 1948, when the Cold War was already in full swing. Until the mid-1950s, fear of a resurgent Germany motivated French policy more than the menace of Stalinist power; hence, the refusal to join a rearmed West Germany in the stillborn European Defense Community (EDC). It was only when the United States and Britain delivered tangible guarantees in the guise of permanent troop deployments on the Continent that France grudgingly acceded to the rearmament of its former nemesis.

What is more, as the Western powers and West Germany concluded their grand bargain of 1954 by which the FRG

---

1. "Revisionist" in this context is meant to transcend the classical definition pertaining to a power in search of territorial change. Rather, the term is intended to characterize an actor that seeks to transform the overall political-strategic status quo in Europe.

regained sovereignty and an army in the framework of NATO, both sides were only too well aware that the alliance was not only to contain the Soviet Union, but also to constrain West Germany. The key idea, recalled British Foreign Secretary Anthony Eden, was to bring "Germany into NATO," but "under the various safeguards which had been devised for her entry into EDC." Those had to be "effective but not too blatant."[2] Hence, the good conduct pledges Bonn had to deliver as price of admission: The FRG foreswore the acquisition of nuclear weapons, integrated its armed forces wholly under NATO command, and promised "never to have recourse to force to achieve the reunification of Germany or the modification of [its] present boundaries."

In addition, the three Western powers put the Federal Republic on notice by underlining the limits of German autonomy. In a joint declaration released on October 3, 1954, the British, French, and American governments declared they would "regard as a threat to their own peace and safety any recourse to force which . . . threatens the integrity and unity of the Atlantic alliance or its defensive purposes." Moreover, they would "consider the offending government as having forfeited its rights to any guarantee and any military assistance." In that case, they would act "with a view to taking other measures which may be appropriate."

That government, though not mentioned by name, was of course the West German one, and the barely veiled threat was military action against German aggression. Until this day, the FRG is not fully sovereign. Though the armies of the occupiers turned into those of allied protectors, the three Western powers retain considerable rights stemming from surrender in 1945, notably those relating to Berlin and Germany as a whole.

Nor was Containment, Part II, just a matter of memory dating back to two world wars during which Germany had twice made a grab for European hegemony. West Germany

---

2. Anthony Eden, *Full Circle* (London: Cassell, 1960), 149–50.

was, in principle, though not in practice, the revisionist power *par excellence*. Its official self-portrayal was that of an incomplete nation; its official teleology was reunification with its "counterstate," the GDR. In none of its actions would the Federal Republic consecrate the territorial amputation inflicted by the Soviet Union on the body of the Reich. Bonn's legal position was that "the final determination of the boundaries of Germany must await . . . a freely negotiated settlement."

Soviet revisionism was even more clearly nontraditional. In the course of World War II, Soviet Russia had acquired all the territory it coveted (the Baltic states, East Prussia, and half of Poland). During the Cold War, the USSR remained revisionist in an underlying, structural sense, that is, fiercely opposed to the order the United States had built on the Western side of the divide. The essential purpose of those institutions, from the Marshall Plan via European economic integration to NATO, was to negate the great advantage embodied in the military potential and geographic position of the Soviet Union. In that respect, the Soviet Union was denied the fruits of victory. With the United States implanted in the European system, Soviet power, though theoretically dominant, was nonetheless devalued to the point of neutralization. Indeed, from a Soviet point of view, real safety was not among the prizes of war, which had destroyed one enemy (Hitler's Germany) only to bring a more formidable foe (the United States) to Russia's doorsteps.

"Structural revisionism," then, was the Soviet postwar destiny—in spite of the great territorial gains amassed until 1945 and the imperial sphere, stretching into the heart of Europe, carved out in the late 1940s. And so, all of Soviet *Westpolitik* thereafter can be subsumed under one overarching imperative: to preempt, undo, or at least weaken the structures of countervailing power the United States had assembled in Western Europe. This is the underlying continuity in not only Stalin's, Khrushchev's, and Bhrezhnev's pressure tactics, but also Mikhail Gorbachev's "new thinking."

The first act in the drama of structural revisionism was the

Berlin Blockade (1948–1949), which has often been interpreted as a grab for all of Germany, but more properly ought to be seen as a last-ditch attempt to reverse West Germany's accelerating amalgamation into the Atlantic coalition. Having come to naught, that gambit was followed by Stalin's notorious neutralization-cum-reunification offer of 1952 that was clearly designed to abort West Germany's rearmament within the European Defense Community. That specific carrot, translating into a Western coalition without Germany, remained in the Soviet arsenal until the FRG was firmly anchored in NATO (1955); thereafter, three decades of Soviet *Westpolitik* followed a strategy of the second-best that aimed to weaken the military potential of the alliance.

Beginning with the Eisenhower administration's "New Look," the core of American power in Western Europe came to be centered on the atom. With the United States holding a quasimonopoly, nuclear weapons were viewed as the most economical means of serving two vital purposes: checking the Soviet Union in the theater of greatest importance to both, while providing, in the guise of "extended deterrence," the glue of America's European alliance. Naturally, Soviet policy on the European chessboard came to be targeted on the "nuclear queen" that dwarfed what was the Soviet Union's by dint of sheer mass and propinquity: a vast conventional and geographical advantage. In the mid-1950s, the Soviet Union first lent its blessing to such denuclearization ventures as the Polish Rapacki Plan and then applied massive pressure against the nuclearization of West German defenses—all the way to unleashing the Berlin Crisis from 1958 to 1962.

The drama was reenacted in the late 1970s—first against the "neutron bomb," then against Pershing II and cruise missiles, and, in each case, the prime target of Soviet diplomacy was West Germany. The latest campaign did not subside until 1987, when the Soviet Union purchased the "double-zero solution" (no land-based nuclear missiles in the range from 500 to 5,000 kilometers) at the price of scrapping all of its own forces in this category. That the Soviet Union was willing to yield about four warheads of its own for each warhead deployed on the Western side offers a powerful testimony to the importance it attaches to denuclearizing West European defenses.

Following the conclusion of the treaty on intermediate-range nuclear forces, Mikhail Gorbachev's "new thinking" returned Soviet declaratory policy to the central goal of the 1950s: the complete denuclearization of Europe. "A European peace order," the general secretary proclaimed during his triumphant state visit to the Federal Republic in the summer of 1989, "does not require nuclear containment, but the containment, indeed, the elimination of nuclear weapons. The issue of the complete elimination of tactical nuclear devices must not be struck from the agenda." This was continuity *par excellence*—but one that did not bear fruit for almost 40 years because an essential condition was lacking: a convergence of interest with Europe's other structural revisionist, the Federal Republic of Germany.

III

In the meantime, West German policy has returned to roots that, unlike those of Soviet antinuclear diplomacy, have long been buried under the postwar rubble, so to speak. For a quarter century, West German diplomacy obeyed—indeed, could not but obey—an ahistorical and antigeographical imperative. After World War II, and for the first time since the creation of the modern German Reich under Bismarck, one part of Germany was in, of, and with the West. In consequence, West German diplomacy remained artificially truncated. *Westpolitik* was virtually all there was, while *Ostpolitik* was suppressed in favor of intimate ties to the United States and then France. Whatever influence, power, and status the Federal Republic sought had to be found in the West, while security had to be achieved against the East. As Konrad Adenauer, chancellor from 1949 to 1963, noted at the beginning of West German foreign policy: "For the German people there is no other way of attaining freedom and equality of rights than . . . in concert with the Allies." This was a remarkable pledge of self-abnegation. But then, self-denial was the very condition of self-assertion in a setting in which even the *right* to have a foreign policy was detained by the three Western occupation powers.

Moreover, by refusing to accept the territorial consequences of World War II, as well as the existence of the GDR, the Federal Republic was saddled with a permanent conflict with the Soviet Union—one that could only be sustained in close alliance with the West. The objective was a classic in the repertoire of client states: to roll West Germany's separate conflict into the general East-West conflict and to identify the threat to one as a threat to all. That made for the greatest historical discontinuity of them all: a junior partnership with the United States in which in exchange for acting as "continental sword," the FRG—paradoxically—earned maximum derivative power through subordination.

Finally, Adenauer did not simply submit to the victors; his policy also reflected an acute sensitivity to the dangers of bipolarity. On the one hand, tight bipolarity suppressed many diplomatic options among clients and patrons alike. On the other, bipolarity always left open one theoretical option to the two great powers, who until recently had been comrades-in-arms: condominial arrangements over the lesser nations in between. Adenauer's enduring nightmare of "Big Twoism" flowed from the second possibility. His horror was the 1945 conference in Potsdam, the Berlin suburb where the United States, the Soviet Union and Britain jointly decided the fate of postwar Germany. Adenauer stated in a radio interview in 1953,

> It is no coincidence that the Soviets keep referring to this agreement again and again. Every Soviet allusion to this agreement constitutes a Soviet invitation to the West to conclude such a bargain at our expense. . . . Bismarck spoke about his nightmare of coalitions. I have my own nightmare: its name is Potsdam. The danger of a collusive great power policy at Germany's peril has existed since 1945. . . . The foreign policy of the Federal Republic has always been aimed at es-

caping from this danger zone. For Germany must not
fall between the grindstones. If it does, it will be lost.

To avoid getting caught between the "grindstones," Adenauer chose unconditional alignment with the West on the
historically confirmed premise that alliance fetters bind both
sides. The choice was deliberate and reflected the chancellor's
reading of circumstances. "One false step," he confided in his
memoirs, "and we would lose the trust of the Western powers.
One false step, and we would be victim of a bargain between
East and West." Or as he recalled once putting it to the American High Commissioner John McCloy: Once Bonn was safely
ensconced in the Western alliance, "the demilitarization and
neutralization of Germany will no longer be possible."

For these three reasons—self-assertion, a separate conflict
with the Soviet Union, and the "nightmare of coalitions"—West
Germany's early foreign policy was in profound conflict with
both the history and geography of modern Germany. No
German entity since the rise of Prussia in the eighteenth
century had ever chosen exclusive ties to, or accepted such
thorough dependence on, the West—quite the contrary. In the
worst of times, Germany and Russia had conspired together
against the West—as at Rapallo in 1922 or with the Hitler-
Stalin pact of 1939. At a minimum, Berlin had fallen back to
reinsurance, heeding Bismarck's advice *"nie den Draht nach St.
Petersburg abreissen zu lassen"* (never to sever the link to St.
Petersburg). And when German leaders shunned that counsel,
they did so at their country's peril—in two world wars.

In historical terms, then, Adenauer's embrace of the West
was abnormal. It was only a matter of time until the Russian
connection would be restored. None other than the most pro-
Western statesman of the Federal Republic, Konrad Adenauer,
laid the foundations for such restoration in 1955—when, hard
on the heels of sovereignty regained, he traveled to Moscow
for the resumption of diplomatic relations. Yet, in the midst of
the Cold War, he sank the seeds into barren soil. Only after 15
years and many an East-West crisis had passed would another

German government, that of Willy Brandt, be able to heed what geopolitical logic had never ceased to demand: the need to recognize the realities of power and, hence, to end West Germany's separate conflict with the East and with it the Federal Republic's excruciating dependence on the West. Conducted in the name of reconciliation, the new *Ostpolitik*, which finally ratified the territorial verdict of World War II, also contained a core of coldly calculated *Realpolitik*.

To sustain the separate conflict over borders and the GDR, Bonn had to buy the loyalty of its allies. To retain their support, it had to submit to the West and forgo options toward the East. Worse, the FRG was stuck with a grating excess demand for security in the face of relentless Soviet hostility—a deficit that could only be "financed" through endless imports of security from the United States. For a middle power that could not possibly counterbalance the Soviet Union on its own, while seeking to escape from dependence on the West (including two economic inferiors, Britain and France), that deficit logically dictated a demand-reduction strategy in the market of security.

The logic that was followed—another classic in the repertoire of client states—is simple enough. To reduce demand for security (and thus dependence), a nation may try to mute, if not resolve, its own conflict with the common adversary. Even while remaining in the original alliance, such a state extends side-payments to the adversary, appeasing the adversary so as to soften its predisposition for threats and pressures. As the foe is given what it might seek to gain by force, the propitiator's demand for alliance loyalty dwindles, while its margin of maneuver widens. Brandt's *Ostpolitik* served precisely that purpose by yielding unto the Soviets what they had tried to exact by bluster and hostility: the acceptance of postwar borders and the all-but-legal recognition of the GDR, paving the road to diplomatic access in all of Eastern Europe.

The bargain with the East, executed between 1969 and 1973, fell far short of a diplomatic revolution, but it amounted to a momentous transformation nonetheless. "At best you can stand on one leg, but you can't walk on it," was the terse diagnosis of the Social Democratic floor leader, Herbert Wehner. The acquisition of a "second leg," ending the artificial truncation of diplomacy after a quarter century of self-denial, would allow not only for mobility in the East, but also relieve pressure on the FRG's "Western leg." Elaborating before the *Bundestag* in July 1975, Chancellor Helmut Schmidt proclaimed: The Eastern treaties "had largely . . . liberated our country from its role as a client." Moreover, "our treaties with Moscow, Warsaw, East Berlin [and] the Four-Power Agreement [on Berlin] have greatly reduced the many reasons . . . for seeking and begging for continuous reassurance." And so, "our margin of maneuver has been extraordinarily enlarged."

IV

The quest for reduced dependence and increased options drives the diplomacy of any state—and it did so all the more in the case of West Germany, which could only regain autonomy by encasing it in the Western coalition. But the drama of *Germania rediviva* ends neither in 1955 (when sovereignty was restored) nor in 1975 (when the cornerstones of the new *Ostpolitik* were in place). The bargains with the West and the East were but prologues. Still waiting to be tackled was the greatest task of them all—the transformation of the stage. And that task is still far from completed, even after Germany's virtual reunification on July 1, 1990.[3]

What was the nature of the stage on which the Federal Republic had to act until Gorbachev's Soviet Union unleashed the East European revolutions of 1989? How will this stage change in the future? Some 40 years after bipolarity descended on Europe, the basics were still in place. The strategic presence of Europe's once remote flanking powers had endured; their military might still extended into the heart of the Continent,

---

3. On that day, all internal borders between FRG and GDR fell, as monetary, economic, and social union was installed.

although it had become more difficult to cement the partition of Germany in a divided Europe. The counterpart of an imposed empire in the East was a "voluntary empire" in the West, upheld by the deference of West European nations to the United States, their "security lender of the last resort." Yet, on both sides of the divide, even "muted" bipolarity spelled dependence assumed and options forgone.

After the revolutions of 1989, the essential role of the two Germanys, already united de facto soon to become one de jure, has thus far changed little. The two parts of Germany still act as the locus for the forward-projection of American and Soviet power. What had changed, even before the momentous transformation of Europe in 1989, was the ledger of costs and benefits. Though its price was partition and submission, bipolarity had conferred enormous benefits on both German states. Instead of dismemberment, there was dual statehood. Instead of a super-Versailles, there was the offer of community with the victors. Instead of indefinite subjection, there was speedy rehabilitation in alliances that extended to both Germanys a shelter and a role. To the Federal Republic, the bargain also offered rich economic rewards. For markets lost in the East, it gained a far more profitable free-trade system in the West that fostered economic growth and buttressed the democratic miracle of the Second German Republic. By 1955, in short, Adenauer had done even better for West Germany than had Talleyrand for vanquished France in 1815.

The profits clearly dwarfed the price—but not forever. By the 1980s, the gains had been absorbed, while the burden had remained—and become all the more grating because, with the postwar generation of leaders on the way out, the prodigious profits of yesteryear had disappeared into the mist of history. "Why can't we be like everyone else?" became the question posed across the entire political spectrum. Thus, what remains today is a nation that, although reunified, cannot settle its own fate as long as the remnants of the postwar system remain in place: hundreds of thousands of foreign troops and thousands of nuclear weapons over which the Germans have little control.

Finally, there are sundry restraints on German sovereignty that are no longer so obviously balanced by the benefits of community.

Even before the revolutions of 1989, (West) German foreign policy was beholden to a long-postponed revisionist impetus analogous to Russia's. Both actors had to operate on a stage that was designed to contain their energies—explicitly in the case of the Soviet Union, implicitly in the case of the Federal Republic. And so, "structural revisionism" was the key to understanding the foreign policies of both powers in the 1980s—as it will be in the 1990s. Both must seek to transcend much of what bipolarity has wrought, and for both the problem is how to improve their position in Europe without losing all the benefits of the *ancien système*.[4]

V

Half a decade into Mikhail Gorbachev's tenure, a triple-revolution in Soviet policy has become evident. First, there has been the shift from "guns" to "butter" in order not only to satisfy long-suppressed civilian demands, but also to turn the Soviet Union from an "Upper Volta with nuclear weapons" (to borrow Helmut Schmidt's famous phrase) into an at least second-rate economy that will not be hopelessly outclassed by the West. Second, there has been fitful progress toward democratization and market-oriented economic reform. Third, there has been the attempt to return to the community of responsible great powers that revolutionary Russia abandoned in 1917. To

---

4. Neither the symmetry of conditions nor the convergence of interests ought to be carried too far for the sake of analytical neatness. The differences are obvious enough. To Germany, the Soviet Union presents not just a partner in system transformation, but also an enduring security threat. Similarly, the USSR retains an abiding interest in containing German power even as it tries to manipulate it to weaken America's position. Hence, to counterbalance each other, neither the Soviet Union nor the United Germany Republic will lightly foresake its American connection.

ease all three departures, the axe was put to the unbearable financial and political costs of empire: from Afghanistan to Angola, from Eastern Europe, where former satrapies were invited choose their own way out of socialism, to Western Europe, where the Soviet Union, once the threatening shadow, began to offer itself as partner in cooperation and radical disarmament.

Still, great powers, even diminished great powers like the Soviet Union, have great permanent interests, and these have by no means disappeared from Russia's books; moreover, it is difficult to see how they could in the face of an immutable strategic geography. The Soviet Union must still counterbalance its only deadly rival, the United States, and in the classic theater of the Cold War, in Europe, it must seek at a minimum to neutralize threats implicit in three possible futures: One is an "Atlantic Europe" that acts as a forward bastion and springboard of American power. The second is a "Devolutionary Europe" that evolves into an autonomous security threat by channeling its mighty economic and demographic resources in a commensurate military potential. The third is a "Revolutionary Europe" in the East that, having shed its bonds and moved into the orbit of West European or German economic power, no longer serves as a security glacis for the Soviet Union.

The tasks imposed by these three threats are virtually regime-independent; they bid the Soviet Union, whatever its composition and constitution, to stave off threats to its power and position. But it is not foreordained that the new moderation in the tone and thrust of Soviet diplomacy equals a commitment to the status quo. Even in periods of retrenchment and recuperation, great powers do not renounce the quest for relative gain and neither has the Soviet Union. One goal of the new regime is obvious: to harness Western Europe's impressive financial and technological assets to the herculean task of Soviet economic development. The other objectives are more properly political, conducing to the formation of a *milieu* that would transcend, or at least modify, the postwar setting in Moscow's favor.

That purpose, of course, dates back to 1945. But the novelty is that the latest of Stalin's successors finally understood, and came to act upon, an ancient piece of sociological wisdom: Enemies create and maintain each other's organizations—and, thus, the status quo. Instead of pressure and armament, the post-1985 Soviet leadership has offered to Western Europe a vision of cooperation, democratic reform, and wholesale disarmament. By 1989, having lost his bet on reforming (as opposed to relinquishing) East European communism, Gorbachev had already changed the status quo toward something more benign and promising than anything Europe has known since World War II. Yet, for all the self-containment of Soviet power, there is still Soviet-Russian reason of state, which cannot be gainsaid and which bids the Soviet Union to improve a Continental position that has been diminished for so long by American power above all.

Soviet reason of state informs a strategy aimed at weakening the American hold in Europe—but not too much. Even competition-conscious Soviet policymakers have come to concede that America-in-Europe is a factor of stability that serves Soviet interests, too. Still, Soviet strategy must follow the well-worn path toward Europe's denuclearization, a course that advances two purposes at once. On the one hand, it would revalue the Soviet Union's conventional and geographical advantage—even with drastic conventional disarmament numerical parity at lower levels could not blunt the God-given edge that is Russia's by dint of geography and sheer mass. On the other hand, Continental denuclearization will sever the most powerful tie that binds Western Europe to its transatlantic patron—as well as what has heretofore been an indispensable safeguard of European security. With or without theater weapons, the Soviet Union will always remain a great nuclear power, with nuclear options aplenty.

Indeed, the claim of military security must be muted altogether. Evidently, one hope is that fewer swords will make for more plowshares. But the political effects might be even more impressive, especially if they prompt Western Europe to relax its guard and to seek safety not in arms and alliance, but in stable politico-economic cooperation within a "pan-European security system." With the Warsaw Pact but a shell and military requirements down, can NATO survive as an effective military coalition? Precisely because the Soviet empire in Eastern Europe collapsed in 1989–1990, the focus of the Soviet grand strategy must shift to Western Europe. And that requires recruiting the West Europeans as tacit allies in stability and cooperation. The prize for the West Europeans, and especially the Germans, is the re-fusion of Europe along the Elbe River, but the price is no less evident: deference toward Soviet sensitivities. If Gorbachev and successors can pull this off, the rewards will be handsome: maximal Soviet influence in all of Europe, which will more than compensate for the loss of Moscow's East European fiefdoms.

VI

Like the FRG before, reunified Germany today plays—indeed, cannot help but play—a starring role in this script. The FRG was the very pillar of an "Atlantic Europe"—the forward bastion of American power after 1945. It hosted not only the bulk of American conventional forces in Europe, but also successive generations of nuclear weapons. Many of these weapons threatened the Soviet "sanctuary," and so they were the target of unmitigated Soviet hostility. With the "double-zero" solution enshrined in the Washington Agreement of 1987, the land-based nuclear threat was contractually banished. The logic of its traditional policy now bids the Soviet Union to get rid of the rest and certainly to forestall compensation through follow-on systems like an airborne stand-off weapon. Because modernization will stand or fall in West Germany, Soviet policy under Gorbachev has been busy since 1987 to confront Bonn with the nasty consequences of such a decision. By the end of the 1980s, Lance modernization was dead, and nuclear artillery on the way out—thanks, above all, to steady German opposition to both.

Nor is it just Soviet pressure and domestic disaffection that has made for a convergence between Soviet and German policy in matters nuclear—another portentous trend coming to maturity in the late 1980s. The Soviet Union has always fought against the nuclearization of Western defenses in Europe, but until the early 1980s it had run up just as regularly against an impenetrable Maginot Line that was West Germany. Yet by the end of the decade, the very center-right government that had put its survival on the line by pushing through the INF deployment, had moved to the vanguard of anti-nuclearism—balking (successfully) against modernization of short-range nuclear forces (SNF) and urging its allies to dispense with nuclear artillery, too.

Why? Among the many dependencies that tied Bonn to the American-sponsored postwar order, none has been tighter than West Germany's reliance on extended deterrence. Because, like the Federal Republic, a united Germany cannot realistically reach for an independent deterrent, it follows that nuclear weapons must lose their exalted role in the European balance if sovereignty and independence are to have real meaning. Denuclearization of deterrence would offer three advantages: First, the demotion of nuclear deterrence would reduce dependence on the United States. Second, it would remove Bonn–Berlin from the hot seat of Soviet pressure, which it has occupied since the mid-1950s. Third, it would devalue the special badge of nuclear status retained by Britain and France and thus their only claim to precedence over Germany.

With "Atlantic Europe," Moscow's nemesis, waning, what are the prospects of a "Devolutionary Europe" where the European nuclear powers, Britain and France, would extend their "umbrellas" to the rest? That outcome is hardly on the horizon of political reality, and so the task of preemption does not enjoy the immediate attention of Soviet diplomacy.[5]

---

5. I have argued the low probability of this case in *The Limited Partnership: Europe, the United States and the Burdens of Alliance* (Cambridge: Ballinger, 1987, especially chapter 5, "Alliance as Order."

Nonetheless, the Soviet Union will not look kindly on a Western Europe that, having been stripped of U.S. nuclear weapons, begins to gestate into a nuclear-armed superstate. In this scenario, too, Germany would be the target of opportunity, as the state that has much to ask from the Soviet Union and, hence, much to lose from downward-spiraling relations. Just prior to economic-monetary union with the GDR on July 1, 1990, the FRG extended $3 billion in credit to the Soviet Union, while persuading the European Community to follow suit. The deal was implicit, but obvious: Economic emoluments were proffered as compensation for the withdrawal of Soviet forces from East Germany. That relationship will surely continue, with Germany playing the part of financier and broker of Soviet interests in European councils, as the EC moves toward "1992" and beyond.

A "Revolutionary Europe," meaning not only the complete collapse of the Warsaw Pact but, subsequently, anti-Soviet regimes throughout Eastern Europe is a nightmare of Russian policy that Bonn–Berlin cannot contemplate with glee. Reunited Germany's key interest will be the complete withdrawal of Soviet troops (380,000 troops in 1990) from the area between the Elbe and Oder-Neisse rivers. To achieve this will require more than just billions of deutsche marks. When de facto reunification began in the fall of 1989, West German policy-makers were quicker than their counterparts everywhere else to speculate about two additional types of compensation. One would be a "different" NATO, that is, a Western alliance so disarmed that it would neither threaten the Soviet Union nor act as a magnet for Hungary, Poland, and Czechoslovakia. The other would be a "pan-European security system" that would simply do away with NATO over time. In such a system, an East European realignment option would not even emerge. And the Soviet Union would not end up looking like the great loser of the Cold War, but as coguarantor of the new order.

As to Eastern Europe proper, Germany's nightmare is not so different from Russia's. Because only a reassured Russia could withdraw behind the Bug, the area in between must continue to serve as a security glacis for the Soviets—which is incompatible with the emergence of pro-Western or anti-Soviet regimes. And because Bonn dreads nothing more than a return to pre-Gorbachev policies (which could halt the Soviet withdrawal, reverse democratization, and harden Moscow's military stance), there is an implicit community of interests between Germany and Russia that recalls the nineteenth-century Bismarckian and post-World War I Weimar precedents. In both periods, Germany and Russia collaborated against East European nationalism. An analogous German policy in the future could consist of two parts: economic expansion into Eastern Europe, but with a scrupulous refusal to challenge Russian security interests. In the process, German diplomacy presumably would work hard to persuade Warsaw, Prague, and Hungary not to move too fast or too far toward the West European sphere.

Such a logic is hardly alien to German policymakers. Before the Great Thaw, Bonn's behavior reflected its fear that an outbreak of violence would beget violent recentralization. During the Polish crisis of 1980–1981, an anonymous adviser to Chancellor Helmut Schmidt put it thus: "If the Russians invade, everything is kaput," thus encapsulating the driving assumption of West German *Ostpolitik*. Because Moscow was the ultimate arbiter of evolution in Eastern Europe, the Soviet Union must be reassured—even to the point where *Ostpolitik* becomes a silent partner in the maintenance of Soviet influence. This is why the Schmidt government was not enthusiastic about Poland's *Solidarity* labor movement and why the chancellor obsessively tried to hold off Western sanctions. During Gorbachev's emotional reception in West Germany in 1989, the general secretary admonished Chancellor Kohl that the pace of reform in Eastern Europe hinged on the proper behavior of the West. And Schmidt's Conservative successor vowed that Bonn would eschew any destabilization.[6] Behind all this was, and is, the premise and paradox of all of West German *Ostpolitik*: "The status quo [in Eastern Europe] must be consolidated so that it may change."[7]

But how? For Germany, the ideal situation would be a maximal security insurance in the West and maximal access-cum-evolution in the East, but it cannot have both. The first objective implies tight alliance ties, as well as high armament levels, which would reestablish precisely the dependence *Ostpolitik* was designed to unshoulder. In addition, German society, as every new poll confirms with ever more dramatic numbers, is no longer willing to carry yesterday's military burden into the future—be it nuclear weapons stationed on German soil, long terms of military service, a large *Bundeswehr*, or the environmental toll of allied forces. Finally, centralization in the West would collide mercilessly with bloc transcendence in the East.

Hence, the underlying logic of West German policy bids Bonn ultimately to solve the dilemma by cracking it in favor of a different diplomatic and military milieu. The task is the "subtle subversion" of bipolarity—doing away with its restraints without pushing in the walls. It proceeds from the inference that because bipolarity—the competitive intrusion of the two superpowers into the heart of Europe—divided Germany and the Continent, the parts can only be fused *pari passu* with the retraction of Soviet power. But because the Soviet Union must be compensated, the United States and NATO cannot be allowed to inherit what the Soviet Union has relinquished. The ultimate goal of German policy, it follows, must be to construct a "European peace order that will overarch and

---

6. In a confidential conversation between Kohl and Gorbachev, as leaked to, and reported in, the West German press.

7. Heinz Rapp, a member of the Social Democratic Party's Commission on Basic Values, in Heinz Rapp, *"Das Kriegsrecht in Polen und die Seele der SPD,"* *Vorwärts,* February 4, 1982.

finally overcome the [two] power blocs."[8] Such a goal, of course, is not very different from Soviet policy that, to undo NATO, first began to push a pan-European security system in the late 1950s and returned to this theme with a vengeance once it became clear that the Muscovite empire in Eastern Europe was beyond salvation.

VII

How can "the two power blocs be overcome?" More precisely, how can the West Europeans and, above all, Germans, dispense with their transatlantic patron while providing the Soviet Union with an incentive to pull out and stay out? It cannot be done by "devolution," by replacing the United States with a nuclear-armed European superstate—for that would merely replicate the Soviet security problem *à l'européenne*. The alternative, the underlying logic of contemporary German "grand strategy," involves the relentless reassurance and propitiation of the Soviets.

Fitful at first, the basic strategy was launched as early as 1969 when Willy Brandt's *Ostpolitik* ended 20 years of almost exclusive preoccupation with *Westpolitik*. As it has evolved, the strategy contains three parts. First, the Soviet Union had to be assured of its political and territorial possessions, recognition of which was formalized in the "Eastern Treaties" from 1970 to 1973. The status quo had to be consecrated so that it might change. Second, territorial stability in the East had to be buttressed with regime stability on the premise that reassured rulers will also be relaxed rulers. Unless it could count on staying in the driver's seat, the Soviet Union would not loosen the reins at home and in Eastern Europe. Seeing its glacis

---

8. The goal was first announced in the Government Program of the Social Democratic Party of Germany for 1987-1990 that was published October 1986. Three years later, the term "European peace order" was also used by Helmut Kohl, the Christian-Democrat chancellor, in the Common Declaration signed by Kohl and Gorbachev on the occasion of the latter's state visit.

secure and unchallenged, however, Moscow could lengthen the imperial leash. Its cohorts would then enjoy greater autonomy with respect to both domestic liberalization and diplomatic movement. And this would set in motion a "virtuous circle"—-with reforms breeding domestic consent and legitimacy allowing for ever more reforms, but minus the risk of domestic explosions.

Whence it followed, third, that East-West confrontation was the deadly bane of bipolarity's "subtle subversion." Continued confrontation and Cold War would lead to regime insecurity, allowing Moscow to brandish the external threat as tool of bloc discipline and forcing the regimes to tighten the leash at home. At a minimum, confrontation would redound to the hardliners, enhancing their power against their reform-minded comrades. Worse, sharpened rivalry between the great, raising the voice of security, would strengthen their hold over the small and compress their margins of maneuver in the process.

This is why, during Cold War II in the early 1980s, the Schmidt government fought tooth and nail to keep the rising tide of superpower strife away from Europe—why he tried to evade economic sanctions against the Soviet Union, why he pleaded with Bhrezhnev to reverse the SS-20 buildup so that he could avoid counterdeployment with cruise and Pershing II missiles. The second Cold War, by threatening to refreeze what détente and *Ostpolitik* had so painstakingly unthawed, would inevitably inflict the heaviest penalties on the FRG. And West Germany would suffer twice—both as state and as half-nation because the fortunes of both are so thoroughly tied to a benign East-West climate in Europe. As Schmidt put it in 1980, "we cannot afford gestures of strength [against the Soviet Union]."

Nor has the logic of *Ostpolitik* lost its hold just because the Berlin Wall has crumbled along with the Soviet empire in Eastern Europe. Reassurance must still inform German policy as long as the Russians are ensconced between the Elbe and Oder-Neisse rivers. (In July 1990, Gorbachev promised a pullout "within three to four years.") Thereafter, reassurance must continue to operate because a domesticated Soviet Union might always be tempted to return to the nasty ways of yore, in which case Germany might be thrown back to its earlier dependence on the West. Yet at that point, "the West" might no longer spell security underwritten by a functioning alliance, but merely a geographical concept. This leads to the deepest layer of German "grand strategy": the sources of influence commanded by a middle power with the specific handicaps of West Germany.

Germany's outstanding assets are its economic potential and geographic position. Both, however, were devalued by the legacies of World War II and by the European order built thereafter. To be sure, that order initially provided ample and unexpected benefits to the war's defeated powers. Yet, the vast wealth accumulated under the new international regime could not be converted, at least not at favorable exchange rates, into other forms of power. With the Iron Curtain in place, West German economic prowess could not buy political influence in the East—a traditional outlet for German energies. Nor could wealth be converted into military strength above and beyond what limited autonomy (and historical memories) allowed. Surely, West Germany has the resources to build a first-class nuclear deterrent; yet, it does not do so by dint of imposed renunciation and political good sense.

Germany's critical position in the heart of the Continent, which enabled Bismarck to manage European diplomacy from the center, was similarly constrained by the postwar order. Integration in the West simultaneously harnessed and neutralized West Germany's assets. Fused to the West and barred from the East, the Federal Republic was welded into place, so to speak. Its separate conflict with the East compounded the problem. But even after partial emancipation through the new *Ostpolitik*, even after the decline of bipolarity, the system remained destiny. Until this day, Germany cannot assure military security on its own; until this day, it has no serious options beyond alliance with the West.

The dominant feature of the postwar system was an

extraordinary web of military arrangements that tied down each and all, but none more than the two Germanys. Though originally the greatest profiteers of the Cold War (there was suddenly life after total defeat), the two German states also turned into militarized bipolarity's greatest victims—trapped in dependence and constraints. When the system's strictures fell away, reunification became reality. But this is hardly the end of the story. As long as the necessity of guaranteeing security for and against Germany continues to raise its stern face, dependence on, and deference to, surrounding powers will still claim its due. This implies that Mars, the father and guarantor of the *ancien régime*, must be dethroned for good if Germany is to come into its own. Only to the extent to which the imperatives of military security are loosened or pushed off center stage can the unique economic, geographic, and diplomatic assets of Germany be fully exploited. Why so?

Imagine, for instance, a postbipolar system that so constrained Moscow's military power and geographic advantage that demand for military security in Western Europe would decline to a fraction of the postwar level. Not that this is the most realistic of bets, but one can conceive of a minimum strategic deterrent held in check by an analogous arsenal on the U.S. side, the scrapping of all theater nuclear weapons, and the withdrawal of all Soviet troops behind the Bug combined with a radical drawdown of Soviet conventional forces west of the Urals—all complemented by intrusive verification, constraints on mobility and offensive weaponry, and a demonstrably defensive deployment and training of remaining forces. This would be a giant step toward a military balance that might obviate the need for counteraggregation in the West and provide a setting in which Germany could at least begin to think about life after alliance, heretofore the most serious drain on its autonomy.

Imagine, further, a setting in which the currency of military power has been drastically devalued and with it the foremost traditional source of Soviet influence. It follows that the value of other currencies of power would rise in tandem. For now, and into the third millennium, the Soviet Union will remain a sickly economy with an insatiable demand for financial and technological infusion. Apart from the United States and Japan, it is Germany that has the requisite wherewithal—and a double-advantage, to boot. Unlike Japan, it is neither chained to the American market nor held down by stultifying territorial demands (over the Kurile Islands). Unlike the United States, Germany is not an existential rival of the Soviet Union, and its historical reputation for economic excellence is a living legend in the East.

In an economic game no longer overshadowed by vast disparities in usable military strength, Germany would no longer need to defer to allies for strategic reasons. At the same time, it could treat with the Soviet Union as an equal, indeed, as a superior player. The chips commanded at the economic table could be invested, though not without transaction costs, in the political game in which economic emoluments would buy diplomatic leverage both in the East and in the West. Diplomatic leverage would come from playing the man in the middle. Representing Soviet interests in Western economic councils, Germany would act as the prime interlocutor of the Soviet Union. By the same token, a special relationship with Moscow would enhance Germany's weight in the West. Cooperating with and reassuring either side, while committing itself completely to neither, Germany would become in-dispensable for both.

Whatever the actual variations, it is visions such as these that inform contemporary German reason of state. *Raison d'état* bids Bonn–Berlin to unshoulder the strictures of the *ancien système* and to revalue the unique, "civilian" sources of its power. An even older reason of state bids Germany to secure its vulnerable position in the middle by playing off the flanks so as to keep them from joining against the center. This was the policy of Bismarck and the aim of Gustav Stresemann during the short-lived Weimar Republic. Of course, the new Germany—solidly rooted in liberal democracy—bears no resemblance to its Wilhelmine and Weimar predecessors. But geography, alas, does *not* change, and precisely because life in the middle is fraught with danger, it creates the impetus to transmute a strategic liability into a diplomatic asset. And so contemporary German diplomacy will surely take a page out of the book written before and after the reign of Kaiser Wilhelm II. For a while, Bismarck actually did manage to control East-West relations from Berlin, and Stresemann aspired to that role by cooperating with the West while simultaneously building a special relationship with Soviet Russia.

If these assumptions are correct, then Germany and the Soviet Union are, willy-nilly, natural partners in system transformation. For their own reasons, both want to dismantle the structures of bipolarity—but neither too fast nor too thoroughly. Too much transformation in the East, culminating in anti-Soviet regimes, is a threat to Moscow's status and security, but this is all the more reason for the USSR to harness German "revisionism" within a reliable partnership. Too much transformation in the West, accelerating the decline of the Atlantic Alliance, is a threat to German security, but this, too, is all the more reason for the Germans to propitiate the Soviet Union and to domesticate Soviet power within a milieu no longer dominated by the force of arms.

VIII

Objectively, the convergence of Soviet and German diplomacy in the 1990s is conditioned by several factors. Above all, reunited Germany must evacuate 380,000 Soviet troops ensconced on the territory of the former GDR. Ideally, this would be done by buying Moscow's consent to Germany-in-NATO. That would reassure all of Bonn–Berlin's traditional allies, and Moscow's former satrapies as well. But, in practice, such an outcome will require hefty compensation. One form of compensation is material, involving large transfers of money and technology. Another is long-term deference to the great power claims of the Soviet Union. A third form of compensation may be a NATO so transformed by denuclearization and disarmament that it bears little resemblance to the alliance as we have known it since 1949. A fourth could be a different security system altogether—one in which both Cold War alliances would be subsumed in a pan-European architecture.

For the Soviet Union, the entire process ideally would culminate in "Pan-Europe." The transcendence of alliances would be the ultimate payoff because it would yield what Moscow has cherished since the early 1950s: a system no longer dominated by its existential rival, the United States. (And in the shorter term, it would allow for withdrawal without loss of face.) The logic of German reason of state pushes in the same direction for different reasons. The end of alliance would spell the end of dependence and the liberation of Germany's unique, "civilian" sources of influence. Yet, this is but the ideal; the dilemmas are hardly less obvious.

The most grating problem is that "pan-Europe," also known as the Conference on Security in Europe or Helsinki Process would be a reversion to the hapless "collective security" mechanism of the League of Nations. The key idea of "collective security" is the absence, indeed, the prohibition, of fixed alliances and their replacement by the obligation of each and all to come to the aid of whoever is attacked or threatened. Would-be aggressors and intended victims would be members in one and the same club. The problem is that this lofty idea has never worked. When there was effective action, it was not collective—for example, in the case of the UN's 1950 "Uniting for Peace" resolution, which was but a "collective security" cover for an American-led coalition against North Korea. And when there was universality, it did not produce security—as in the case of the League's watery sanctions against fascist Italy in support of Abyssinia in 1935.

Nor is there any conceptual reason to assume that such a system could produce security—except in one very limited case that is actually irrelevant. If all the great powers want peace, then there will be peace. But in that case, it would not be the collective security mechanism that produced security, but the common adherence to the status quo of those capable of undermining it. (An example—actually, a tautology—might be the Concert of Europe in the wake of the Napoleonic Wars when there was peace because none of the great powers desired war.) In other words, under such special circumstances the mechanism "works" because it need not work. If there is stability, there will be security—with or without a League of Nations–type system of peacekeeping.

In all other cases, it ought to be assumed that nations will not sacrifice their selfish interests on the altar of abstract justice—which is precisely what has happened in the long, but hapless history of UN peacekeeping. Whenever the great powers or their clients were involved in war, the conflict split the international community instead of harnessing each and all against the presumed aggressor. Instead of overcoming the natural trend toward alignment and counter-alignment, the system inevitably produced a bipolar outcome. In addition, neither the League nor the UN has ever been able to come up with a satisfactory definition of "aggression," the indispensable precondition of collective action. In short, collective security requires nations to behave so virtuously as to make the mechanism unnecessary.

Possibly, but only possibly, an institutionalized CSCE could act as guardian of stability on the periphery—for example, in the case of hostility between Hungary and Romania. But if, say, the Soviet Union were involved, confronting the members of a would-be *posse comitatus* with vast risks, the mechanism would fall apart. Moreover, the nuclear age has added an existential risk that would reduce any collective security system to a grandiose nothing. If even tried and true friends are loath to unsheathe their nuclear sword on behalf of allies, as critics of extended deterrence assert, how would they ever court nuclear suicide on behalf of an abstract principle?

This is why German dreams of building security by "transcending the alliances" are bound to remain but dreams. A "pan-European security system" *assumes* security; it cannot create it. Hence, the irreducible limits to any long-term collaboration between Germany and Russia. As long as Germany does not go for a sophisticated second-strike capability, it must either accept Russian strategic primacy or rely on an alliance with the only power capable of deterring the Soviet Union—which is the United States. Nor can Germany, no matter how potent economically, dispense with the secondary alliance that is the European Community—at once indispensable to its economic well-being and a fallback position in the event that the United States washes its hands of Western Europe. Finally, there is no solace to be drawn from the troubled history of Russo-German relations. True, when Russians and Germans have not been at each other's throats, they sometimes have collaborated with one another. But even then they have tried to weaken and undermine each other. There was attraction, but also just as much repellence, ending more often than not in bloody war. If history is a guide, then Germans and Russians are not the ideal co-managers of European order.

So, even as reunification is completed along with the withdrawal of Soviet troops from Central Europe, Germany is not as free as it might wish to be. Nor will the Soviet Union (or whatever replaces it) ever be completely out of the European system. Contemporary Russia, at least two-fifths of it, *is* in Europe. And no matter how chastened or democratic, even a diminished Russia (the USSR minus its multinational empire), it will still be the largest country on earth.

For all these reasons, the demise of the bipolar postwar order does not spell the end of Europe's traditional security problem: the dynamism of Germany and the might of Soviet Russia. Both powers must still try to contain each other even as they collaborate. And Germany, the smaller of the revisionist duo, must still rely on others for insurance—all the more so because only a Germany harnessed to a functioning Western community can stifle *ex ante* the anxieties of its friends and neighbors that an unfettered Germany would inevitably raise. Sheer prudence (and postwar experience) also forbid Germany to seek security from a solitary perch in the middle.

The contemporary European game favors Germany precisely because its rules are determined by welfare rather than warfare. As long as the accounts are not settled with "blood and iron," but with capital movements, and as long as relative power is not measured with tanks and troops, but with payments surpluses, Germany can count on a starring role on the European stage. Conversely, a Germany that tried to convert economic into military clout, or worse, aspire to a nuclear panoply, would risk recreating precisely those hostile coalitions that proved Germany's undoing in two world wars.

Community, then, appears to be an abiding imperative of Germany's foreign policy. One secret of Europe's astounding stability after two murderous world wars has been the harmonious domestication of West German energies—through a blend of constraint and community. That prescription still embodies the counsel of wisdom, certainly for those Germans who have learned from bitter historical experience that isolation is neither splendid nor serendipitous—and, even more, that self-containment is a condition of self-assertion.

The continuities of post-postwar Europe also include the reality that neither Germany, nor indeed all of Europe, can dispense with the United States. True, the U.S. role will change. American power will no longer convert so easily into influence in a setting in which authority over allies cannot but dwindle in tandem with the Soviet threat. In such a system, some devolution of responsibility and status is unavoidable, and this will inevitably accrue to Germany, the system's strongest member next to the United States and the Soviet Union. On the other hand, neither the sources of American influence, nor the need for them, have dried up. To maintain an American say in the affairs of Europe is not just a narrow American interest; it serves each and all, and, in that sense, the *ancien régime* by no means has become obsolete.

The Germans want the United States in the system because it is their security lender of last resort. France, Britain, and the other West European states want the Americans "in" for the same reason—as a counterweight to German assets and aspirations. Liberated from the short leash of the Stalinist empire, Czechs, Poles, and Hungarians presumably do not want to be left alone in *Zwischeneuropa*, caught between Germany in the West and Russia in the East. For them, too, the United States is a counterweight against both neighbors, especially as a deterrent against re-invasion by the Soviet Union. Even the Russians, though still intent—ideally, by peaceful means—to dominate the Continent, must have an interest in the American presence, as it would maintain some control over their foremost confederate-competitor, that is, Germany.

This perspective would remain valid even in a Europe that moves toward a "counter-realist" paradigm of interstate politics that some have already touted as the Continent's new destiny. Accordingly, all of Europe will eventually obey the rules already operating in Western Europe: Competition for advantage persists, but force is no longer the natural adjunct of policy. Indeed, has not violence been banished already between East and West? Where are the volcanoes of aggressive nationalism that have periodically erupted into a European war? And if democracy spreads all the way to the Urals, will this not finally vindicate the Enlightenment's assertion that only despots make war, while republics are inherently pacific?

Realism bids us to look not at effects, but causes. The sterilization of force in Europe cannot be separated from its persistence. Europe's ultra-stability cannot be abstracted from the great reservoirs of military power—especially nuclear—that have contained and devalued each other. In addition, the more power recedes, the more it will liberate previously suppressed challenges to the old regime—and nowhere more so than in the imposed empire that was Russia's. Will Moscow accept that verdict and contain itself, as it were? In the face of such an uncertain bet, a paid-up military insurance policy on the part of the West remains a minimal counsel of prudence. Finally, even those who aspire to a new paradigm must wish for *controlled* change—lest too much too soon provoke the vengeful return of the old. This is where the basic interests of the two "revisionists" meet with those of the status quo powers—where skillful statecraft can yet rejoin the two halves of Europe without gambling away the precious gift of its stability.

V

Defining "Europe": Purpose Without Commitment?

Simon Serfaty

T HE SUBJECT OF THIS ESSAY is "Europe." Some argue that even if limited to a narrow geographic definition that reduces it to the 12 members of the European Community, "Europe" still remains a fiction. Others insist that it is already a reality. Although both conclusions are exaggerated, neither one is entirely wrong. Indeed, a review of the past 45 years—a period more than twice as long as the entire interwar era (1919-1939)—teaches that, notwithstanding its many false starts and exaggerated dead ends, "Europe" has acquired a significant and largely irreversible reality. That reality does not amount to a truly integrated and supranational body politic, but it extends nonetheless far beyond the sole boundaries of a customs union.

The central characters in the process of European integration are Germany, France, and Great Britain. That France has often held central stage in this process should come as no surprise in light of the constraints imposed by history on a divided Germany and, by geography, on an insular Great Britain. As George Kennan surmised after World War II, "the driving force behind any movement toward political unification on the continent . . . would be, naturally and unquestionably, France."[1] What was true at the start of the Cold War, with the grand initiatives that produced the European Coal and Steel Community, envisioned a European Defense Community, and launched the European Economic Community, is still true as the Cold War comes to an

---

1. George F. Kennan, *Memoirs, 1925-1950* (Boston: Little, Brown, 1977), 455.

end, with new and ambitious projects related to the creation of a single market, the accelerated search for monetary union, and a renewed call for political union.

To be sure, "Europe" can hardly be shaped by any one of its members alone: Any national design for Europe requires support from at least one of the other two leading states of the Community to overcome the likely opposition of the third. Because there has been no French design, whatever its goals, that enjoyed the combined support of Germany and Britain from the start, intra-European discord has shaped every *relance* of the past 40 years. Thus, ever since the special Anglo-French relationship sought in the 1950s was abandoned during the early years of the Fifth Republic, "Europe" has featured a Franco-German *pas de deux* in which the skills of the French ballerina have relied on the strength of her German partner. Now, however, the radical transformation of the European balance of power resulting from the merger of the two German states and the disengagement of one and possibly both superpowers, are likely to require again Britain's active involvement in "Europe" to balance the weight of a reunified Germany.

Not that the complexities of West European unification can be reduced to these three countries only: Also to be considered are the other nine member states—the all-important *corps de ballet* whose contributions, occasionally at center stage or more often from the wings, have also affected and shaped the transformation of the Community. Italy is a case in point, although not the only one. In the 1980s, two of the most significant tests of Atlantic unity and European unity—namely, the decisions to deploy intermediate-range nuclear forces and ratify the Single European Act—were influenced, perhaps decisively, by the Italian government. Yet, because of the many limits it faces at home, Italy's European policy can only be of special significance over one issue at any given time, but not over most issues over a sustained period of time.

Finally, Europe's choreography has often been directed by two characters whose role had been envisioned initially as brief cameo appearances. As will be recalled, the two superpowers were expected to return home quickly following the end of World War II. Instead, each stayed, or claimed to stay, because of the other. Their respective presence on both sides of a divided Europe conditioned the history that followed: In the West, the promises of the American model helped make unification desirable, while the threatening form of the Soviet model helped make it necessary; and, as the evidence of failure in the East mounted, the appeal of the Western political and economic model became increasingly irresistible.

That the two superpowers responsible for Europe's postwar divisions would influence the processes by which these divisions might end should come as no surprise. For more than four decades, the Soviet Union held the key to both of these processes, in the East through the Warsaw Pact and in the West because of Germany. Détentes came and went, but without much evidence that the postwar stalemate might ever be broken: a continent split between two ideological blocs and many national boundaries, including at least two Germanys. In recent years, however, the prospect first, and the fact next, of a Soviet Union so absorbed with its problems at home as to leave it relatively indifferent to changes in its empire abroad and acquiescent to changes in Germany opened a heretofore unthinkable prospect: a weak and divided Russia that, together with the countries of Eastern Europe, dreams of renting some space in the common house built by a strong and uniting Western Europe.

Thus, evidence of change can now be found everywhere: a circumstance as historically unprecedented in the West as it has been politically unthinkable in the East. In Western Europe, the changes caused by progressive integration must come to terms with the questions raised by Germany's unification. In Eastern Europe, the sudden changes surrounding the disintegration of the Soviet empire (from within as well as from without) must come to terms with the issues raised by the political consequences of ideological bankruptcy and economic failure. And between the superpowers, the uncertain changes brought about by the uneven end of their respective hegemonies, and the will to sustain them, must come to terms with the need to preserve their mutual and legitimate interests within a new European security system. These three cycles of change and security in and for Europe overlap. None can move too quickly, none too slowly. If one were to be derailed, or fall out of sync with the other two, all three would be threatened.

II

Throughout the years, the future of "Europe" has been built around, about, or against Germany. After the war, French fears of being separated from, or isolated with, Germany in Europe— even a divided Germany—pushed the policies of the Fourth Republic toward "Europe" and, simultaneously, into an extra-European context that included either one of the two Anglo-Saxon islands of the West (or preferably both), as well as the Soviet Union. Coming after the Anglo-French Treaty, symbolically signed at Dunkirk, French designs for European unity initially relied on close cooperation with Britain, which was expected to serve as a counterweight to a resurgence of German power on the Continent; extended to the United States within the context of the Atlantic Alliance, European unity was supposed to foreclose West Germany's temptation in the East; and absent the temptation of a reunification that would come from the East, France hoped to find in Moscow the best guarantor of Germany's division, an expectation implicit in the agreement signed by de Gaulle and Stalin in December 1944. Thus, the Fourth Republic assumed complementarity between the 1944 Franco-Russian alliance, the 1947 Anglo-French Treaty, and the 1949 North Atlantic Treaty.[2]

---

2. "We considered," wrote de Gaulle in his Memoirs, "that [alliances] would be constructed in three stages: first a Franco-Russian treaty providing for initial security; . . . an agreement still to be made between France and Great Britain constituting a second degree; the future United Nations pact, in which America would play a decisive role crowning the entire edifice and serving as an ultimate recourse." *The Complete Memoirs of Charles de Gaulle* (New York: Simon & Schuster, 1967), 745.

Understood as a necessary factor of compensation for, and protection from, France's own weaknesses and its allies' unreliability, the idea of "Europe" soon emerged as a central feature of a security system against Germany and the two superpowers. In the 1950s, related French schemes still aimed at bringing Britain in Europe (possibly with the same measure of automaticity as had been agreed at Dunkirk), while strengthening the American ties with Europe (through the North Atlantic Treaty that had been signed in Washington in 1949). Neither the failure of the European Defense Community in 1954, nor that of the joint Anglo-French intervention at Suez in 1956, ended Paris' efforts to build Europe with London: In 1957, France still hoped for British participation in the Rome Treaty, and it was Britain's choice to opt out.

Unlike earlier attempts at European unity, however, the Rome Treaty was envisioned as a preliminary step toward the end of the U.S. tutelage. Hence, the importance given by de Gaulle to Harold Macmillan's agreement with President Kennedy at Nassau at the end of 1962, which, in the view of the French president, reasserted America's dominance at the expense of the agreement he had reached with Britain's prime minister a few weeks earlier at Rambouillet. Thus convinced of an Anglo-Saxon collusion aimed at his leadership in Europe, de Gaulle lost no time in denying Britain's membership in the Common Market, and the saga of Britain's entry in Europe was, therefore, extended for another decade.[3] But this renewed demonstration of

---

3. At Rambouillet, remembered de Gaulle, Macmillan offered support for the French nuclear force. "We also have ours," [Macmillan] said, "and we ought to be able to unite the two within a context that would be independent from the United States." But a few weeks later at Nassau, de Gaulle added, "Great Britain gave the United States whatever poor atomic forces she had. She could have given them to Europe. She therefore made her choice." (Quoted in André Passeron, *De Gaulle Parle, 1962-1966* [Paris: Fayard, 1966], 199 and 207.) Not surprisingly, Macmillan's recollections of this meeting are somewhat different. "The General was in no doubt as to my intentions . . . that if the United States administration canceled Skybolt I would try to obtain Polaris in its place." (*At the End of the Day, 1961-1963* [New York: Harper & Row, 1973], 348.) In fact, the

Britain's special relationship with the United States also led in quick succession to the Franco-German Treaty of Friendship, the accelerated construction of the French nuclear deterrent, and the French withdrawal from NATO.

Seen in this light, even de Gaulle cannot be legitimately viewed as a stubborn opponent of European unity, whose need he recognized and sought to advance within a framework that would not impair the sovereignty of the state. To be sure, in a period of French ascendancy, de Gaulle had little use for "Europe," which he envisioned as scarcely more than a series of carefully crafted bargains between nation states in areas of common or complementary interests. Part of this vision—which de Gaulle was hardly the only European (or French) leader to hold—reflected concern about the emergence of a polity in which national bureaucracies and governments would be unable to stop, reverse, or slow down the progressive rejection of the nation-state. By destroying any illusion about the automaticity of this process, and by reaffirming the supreme value of the state against the vision of a supranational Europe—"except for myths, fictions, and pageants"—de Gaulle diluted the federalist dream, of course. But he preserved the Rome treaty, which he had reportedly planned to destroy, by making sure that, whatever the treaty might have said or implied, the need for unanimity rather than majority voting would continue to protect the interests and the values of the state. After de Gaulle's retirement in early 1969, an agreement was reached quickly for the expansion of the Community from six to nine members. But Britain's extended quarrel over the terms of its accession suggests that the General's "No" to Britain's membership was not, after all, a general "No" to "Europe" and its expansion.[4]

Rambouillet and Nassau meetings merely helped de Gaulle justify and explain what he was determined to do anyway.

4. The debate within the British government over membership in the Common Market was settled only after direct pressures from the United States. Thus, according to Macmillan, Kennedy lost no time in trying to

Settlement of the issue of British membership in January 1973 hardly ended the Anglo-French rift in and over Europe, about which the two countries have continued to hold mutually exclusive visions and ambitions. Hostile to the broader implications of the Single European Act, to which she agreed reluctantly, Margaret Thatcher's opposition echoes or parallels the rhetoric and vision presented in a different context by de Gaulle 20 years ago: opposition, that is, to a transfer of sovereignty from elected governments to an "appointed bureaucracy" in Brussels, where decisions imply "some sort of identikit personality . . . France as France, Spain as Spain, Britain as Britain, each with its own customs, traditions and identity." Thatcher's remarks at Bruges on September 20, 1988, would have been applauded by de Gaulle, who liked neither Britain's insularity (which he nevertheless envied at times), nor the British people (whose solidarity under duress he sadly contrasted with the divisions of his own people), but whose obstinacy he shared.[5]

This is not to say that Thatcher's apprehensions are without foundation. For instance, to delay Britain's entry into the rate mechanism of the European Monetary System until the British rate of inflation had moved closer to the average rate in Europe made political sense because of the impact that the EMS might have had otherwise on levels of employment (as was the case in France and other countries of Southern Europe). In de Gaulle's case, too, insisting on the further cohesion of the Six

---

impress upon him "how anxious the Americans were for us to go in the Six. This for two reasons. Economically they thought it would be better for them to deal with one larger group than with two groups; bargaining in tariffs and trade would be easier. Politically, they hoped that if we were in the Six we should be able to steer them and influence them, whatever might be the political personalities." *Pointing the Way, 1959-1961* (New York: Harper & Row, 1972), 350-351.

5. "France with its French, Germany with its Germans, Italy with its Italians," de Gaulle remarked similarly in his press conference of May 15, 1962, when he dismissed the vision of a Europe "thought and written in some integrated Esperanto or Volapuk."

as a prerequisite to enlargement, and on completing the tariff removals called by the Rome Treaty before moving on with other integrationist schemes, was not inappropriate. What has made little or no sense, however, is a tone that has left Thatcher increasingly isolated as a "picky, quibbling laggard" who argues her way into the cul-de-sac of resignation from, and abdication to, the European process that Britain has continuously fought and joined for more than four decades.

The same impression of *déjà vu* is given by the policies of François Mitterrand who resurrected the European policy of the pre-Gaullist years following a bitter debate within the government and his party over the constraints forced upon a Socialist France by the restrictive institutions and practices of the European Monetary System. After three successive devaluations of the French franc between October 1981 and March 1983, Mitterrand opted for stability: A franc kept strong within the confining structure of a German-dominated EMS might cost jobs, which it did, and even growth, which it no longer does; but it would also permit lower inflation and, in the long run, the lower interest rates required for the development of support industries that would reduce French reliance on imported equipment goods. Faced at the time with such other self-reinforcing factors as the evolution of U.S. and German policies as well as the transformation of U.S.-Soviet relations, Mitterrand returned to his earlier European vocation, which had gained him Jean Monnet's support as *"une valeur sure"* in the 1965 presidential elections. "France cannot be France without grandeur," de Gaulle had said. Now, Mitterrand appeared to embrace the more modest vision of a France that could not be France without Europe. Echoes of the Fourth Republic: The European Defense Community sought German soldiers without German Army, a European Monetary Union would rely on the German mark without the *Bundesbank*. Thus, even before events around and within European began to move at a pace that, in Mitterrand's words, "he would not have dared hope for"—and, perhaps, dared not fear either—the French president was placing Germany at the center of a grand strategy designed to move Europe *tous azimuts*.

That this renewed emphasis on the necessity of European unity would coincide with a renewed interest in Atlantic harmony was not unusual. Entering the 1950s, too, failure of the "European" answer to the question of Germany's rearmament led to a quick agreement on a package that featured elements of both a *relance européenne,* with a West European Union (WEU) that included Britain, and a *relance atlantique,* that is, a North Atlantic Alliance opened to West German participation, but patrolled by the United States. Such an approach, it should be noted, had been welcomed by de Gaulle, who had urged earlier that "the enlightened generosity" of the United States "be extended to the realm of defense."[6]

In the 1960s, with the Soviet threat to Europe apparently contained by the evidence of U.S. military superiority (demonstrated most convincingly during the Cuban missile crisis), but with the German threat also muted by the evidence of Soviet hostility to Germany's reunification (and by exaggerated hopes concerning the economic vigor of France), "Europe" could afford to be more directly, and even deliberately, autonomous of Atlantic unity: Accordingly, de Gaulle's opposition to Britain's membership in the Common Market was followed, logically, by his withdrawal from the North Atlantic Treaty Organization. After de Gaulle, clashes between the French vision of European unity under French leadership and the American vision of Atlantic unity under American leadership grew increasingly bitter during the Pompidou presidency, which ended with Foreign Minister Michel Jobert's charges of America's neglect of Europe as "a non-person" and Henry Kissinger's countercharges of Europe's tendency "to elevate the refusal to consult into a principle defining its identity."

Although often maligned in Washington for his tone, Pompidou's successor, Valéry Giscard d'Estaing, introduced significant modifications in the substance of the policies inherited from his two predecessors. Aimed explicitly at improving

6. Quoted in Joseph Barsalou, *La Mal Aimée* (Paris: Plon, 1964), 97.

political relations with both the United States and the Federal Republic, these modifications appeared to devalue the fundamental Gaullist principle of absolute national deterrence within the national sanctuary. More specifically, by making more likely France's early and extensive participation in NATO-directed battlefield actions on West German territory (with conventional as well as with nuclear forces), Giscard brought France closer to the prevailing U.S. flexible-response guidelines for countering Soviet moves against Western Europe. Potentially embarrassing discussions and even arrangements between French armed forces and NATO got under way, including the consideration of plans for acquiring back-up facilities on French soil (available only under specified and restricted conditions).[7]

Although discreetly sought and implemented, Giscard's efforts met with vocal opposition from all political groups in France outside his own small party. Cloaked in a carefully tailored Gaullist mantle, Mitterrand and his allies condemned especially harshly the "extended sanctuary" concept and the prospect of French participation in a battle of Germany, as well as other plans committing France's modern conventional or (particularly) tactical nuclear weapons capability. These plans, critics argued in 1980–1981, would extend the escalation process, detract from national deterrence, and involve France in allied defense planning and defensive actions. In short, on the eve of victory, it appeared that a Socialist regime in France would return to Gaullist strategic and force-structure guidelines and that France's relations with NATO would also move back toward the more explicitly adversarial status carved out by de Gaulle in 1966.

---

7. These points are made and discussed at greater length in Michael Harrison and Simon Serfaty, *A Socialist France and Western Security* (Washington, D.C.: SAIS Occasional Papers in International Affairs, 1981), 27-35. They are developed fully in Michael M. Harrison, *The Reluctant Ally: France and Atlantic Security* (Baltimore: The Johns Hopkins University Press, 1981), especially pages 182-193.

Yet, after he won the 1981 presidential elections, perhaps no less unexpectedly than he had lost the 1978 legislative elections, Mitterrand resumed an Atlantic journey that, whatever its limits, was motivated by the same considerations that had brought him to his first Atlantic vocation in the 1950s: the rise of Soviet military power and the future of Germany. "It seems to me," Mitterrand had noted in the immediate aftermath of the December 1979 dual-track NATO decision to deploy Pershing II and cruise missiles, "that the United States has been able to preserve a worldwide superiority but, in Europe, Soviet superiority is established." Thus, providing support for President Reagan's efforts to achieve a NATO missile deployment helped counter, at no cost to France, the Soviet deployment of SS-20s, whose precision and multiple-warhead capability directly threatened French strategic and industrial targets. But by helping Chancellor Schmidt defeat his own party's opposition to the deployment of new NATO missiles on German soil, Mitterrand also aimed at countering a German drift toward neutralism deemed no less dangerous to the stability of Europe and, hence, the security of France.

Mitterrand's assist, peaking with his celebrated speech at the *Bundestag* in January 1983, was all the more significant as neither he personally, nor his party, or even his country were known for their exaggerated assessments of Soviet military power on behalf of NATO. Well served by this unexpected display of French support (and also that of Italy, where a vote in parliament for deployment ensured German approval in Bonn), but also helped by an increasingly incompetent but dangerous Soviet leadership, the attractive vision of the double-zero proposal on intermediate-range nuclear forces, the impressive performance of the American economy after the brutal recession of 1981–1982, and a well-managed American neglect of transatlantic differences over Third World issues, the INF compromise served as a catalyst for a demonstration of Atlantic unity that had not been seen in a generation. At the Williamsburg summit in 1983, agreement about a wide range of political and economic issues confirmed that the Atlantic discord, which had been amply in evidence during and immediately after the 1982 Versailles summit, had been settled.

The relaunching of Europe that was initiated concomitantly was meant, therefore, to be neither anti-Atlantic nor anti-American. Instead, it was decisively motivated by a desire to emulate the American model—rendered even more appealing by the failure of the Socialist model that the French and other leftist majorities in Europe had nurtured during the many years spent in the opposition. That the drive for unity began to gain momentum in 1982–1985 when President Reagan's America stood at its tallest and when Europe was most troubled by the insufficiency of its own economic performance, especially in the areas of job creation and competitiveness, should, therefore, come as no surprise. To this extent, the push toward European unity had little to do with a "decline" of American power or the "failure" of U.S. foreign policies in the face of a so-called "Gorbachev agenda" that set the tone for a new security system in Europe.[8] On the contrary, coming together with Gorbachev's emphatic acknowledgement of Soviet failures at home and abroad, the broader *relance* written into the implementation of a single European market confirmed that the Cold War was coming to an end on American terms—the terms, that is, that had been outlined 40 years earlier by the Truman administration: a strong and united Western Europe and a liberated Central Europe adding up into the "common European house" that a mellowed Soviet state now hopes to enter.

III

A common European house, if it can be constructed at all, must be built primarily in and around the European Community. On either side of the Atlantic it has been, and it may even remain,

---

8. This point is developed at greater length in the author's *After Reagan: False Starts, Missed Opportunities and New Beginnings* (Washington, DC: The Johns Hopkins Foreign Policy Institute, 1989).

often difficult to take this architecture seriously. With "Europe" pulled forward this way and backward that way, as multistate coalitions shift from issue to issue, the high and melodious tones of greater integration have merged with the low and discordant rumblings of renewed disintegration. Yet, throughout the years, from misstep to misstep and from failure to failure, Europe's architecture has continued to grow.

The idea of "Europe" gained its first institutional formulation in April 1948 with the Organization for European Economic Cooperation (OEEC). The novelty of economic cooperation at the scale that was envisioned by the new organization was striking at the time. Its establishment was neither a matter of ideals nor one of choice, however. It was instead thrust upon a reluctant and largely powerless continent by an assertive and dominant American partner that insisted on the creation of a permanent body able to integrate the area's efforts toward economic recovery. After the U.S. call had been heeded, and the Organization established, it was again a forceful American initiative that thrust upon the OEEC the responsibility of allocating Marshall aid, in spite of London's explicit preference for a looser Atlantic system that would attend to this crucial question from Washington. In short, the functions of the new European organization were specifically tied to the requirements set by Europe's main benefactor on behalf of the Marshall Plan. It was a piece of ad hoc machinery designed to help overcome real divisions among its members to ensure the road to an economic recovery paved with American assistance. But this machinery was also expected to be dismantled soon after such assistance was no longer needed.

The limits of Europe's commitment to its own unification were confirmed by the general irrelevance of the Council of Europe that was organized in 1949: "Of all the international bodies I have known," Paul-Henry Spaak once thundered, "I have never found any more timorous or more impotent."[9] He was not wrong: Notwithstanding its grand rhetoric about the making of a United States of Europe (about which Spaak was one of the few true believers), the Council confined its activities to the marginal or the irrelevant. And although new steps on behalf of "Europe" followed quickly, these steps were not initiated by the Council in Strasbourg, but by the French government in Paris and not because of any commitment to the idea of Europe, but because of old apprehensions about the idea of Germany. For it is there, in Germany, that the French postwar thesis (no German control of its own coal and steel resources), which was dismissed by the United States, and the Anglo-Saxon antithesis (no indefinite discrimination of any Western country), which was widely feared on the Continent, merged to produce the European Coal and Steel Community (ECSC), an imaginative European synthesis calling for the abdication of national control by all members. Barely hidden behind its glowing references to European unity, the French interest in promoting the construction of a supranational authority in a sector of vital relevance to defense policy was unmistakable: to impose irreversible restrictions on the sovereignty of its most persistent adversary in modern times.

Notwithstanding Britain's refusal to join an organization that would be not only European but also supranational, this start was promising. It showed how issues that might not be resolved between the European states could be addressed among them, in the name of a fiction called "Europe." That such a U.S.-sponsored fiction also fostered the Atlantic reality required for the Continent's recovery and security was no small advantage. In September 1950, the French proposal for a European Defense Community (EDC) outlined, therefore, a comparable, though admittedly far more ambitious, compromise between Western needs and European apprehensions

---

9. Quoted in Richard Mayne, *The Recovery of Europe* (New York: Harper & Row, 1970), 169.

about the question of Germany's rearmament. As had been the case with the Coal and Steel Community, "Europe" would provide access to, but deny national control of, needed resources: the German soldiers demanded by the United States on behalf of the West, but without the German Army opposed most openly (but not exclusively) by France in the name of Europe. On the eve of the Cold War, the ideal security system that was envisioned would attend to the double containment of Soviet imperialism and German militarism with two indivisible communities—one Atlantic, the other European, but both Western—which consecrated America as a European power and appeared to finalize Germany's future as a divided country.

For various and complex reasons that need not be discussed here, the European part of that scheme proved unrealistic. After four years of bitter intra-European and transatlantic debates, which centered on Britain's participation and America's guarantees, the EDC was buried at the French National Assembly in August 1954. But, a harbinger of things to come, confusion and despair did not last: In October of that year, the thorny problem of military integration was moved into a West European Union (WEU) where Britain made its most explicit commitment to the defense of Europe while the other states of Europe renewed their commitment to a general Western structure that would be built with, rather than against, a divided Germany that also pledged nuclear abstinence. After the Federal Republic's formal admission into the North Atlantic Treaty Organization in May 1955, the WEU, whose main purpose had been, therefore, to salvage the pretense of European unity for the sake of preserving the reality of Atlantic unity, was promptly forgotten (at least for the next three decades), and the quest for European integration resumed with more modest calls for a common economic market.

In 1957, the Rome Treaty asserted explicitly that the "ever closer union" to which the Treaty committed its six charter members (France and Germany, as well as Italy and the three Benelux countries) could be achieved more effectively with the relatively small steps it proposed than with the politico-military grand designs of previous years. Although the broad terms of the Treaty had been outlined at the Messina summit in June 1955, the document was drafted somewhat hastily to take advantage of a political constellation that appeared relatively stable and favorable (after the French elections of January 1956 and before the German elections in the fall 1957) at a time when the European economies were enjoying a series of so-called miracles.[10] Moreover, with intra-European trade doubled during the six years that followed the establishment of the OEEC, its members were now coming up against monetary and trade barriers that had to be overcome in one way (through OEEC mechanisms, which Britain favored) or the other (a Common Market, which the Europeanists preferred).

Yet, these good reasons notwithstanding, it was the failed Anglo-French intervention in Suez in 1956 that permitted quick ratification in Paris, where the Rome Treaty was approved by the National Assembly after a debate that centered less on its specific terms than on those of the Suez debacle: Threats from Moscow, pressures from Washington, and ridicule in Cairo added up to a demonstration of Europe's impotence that made the case for unity all the more compelling. Overcoming such impotence was made even more significant and urgent as the Anglo-French intervention in Suez coincided with the Soviet intervention in Hungary (where the assertiveness shown by the Eisenhower administration vis-à-vis its main Western allies was hardly matched vis-à-vis its main adversary in the East). Yet, whatever political objectives and ambitions might have shaped the inner logic of the Rome Treaty, the European Community it envisioned was kept

---

10. The mean rate of increase in industrial production in the original Six amounted to 8 percent from 1950 to 1953, and 10 percent from 1953 to 1956: To a large extent, it was such vigorous economic performance that made entry in the Common Market possible, and not the other way around. See Sidney Dell, *Trade Blocs and Common Markets* (New York: Alfred A. Knopf, 1963), 108.

specifically economic: a common market free of trade barriers, and in which goods, services, labor, and capital would move without hindrance among the member states.

The history of European economic integration that was launched with the Rome Treaty began as it was to unfold subsequently: Everything was to be negotiable, including everything that had already been negotiated. Hence, perhaps, the skepticism that was shown toward the new European *relance*: Within a few months, states that had opted for membership already acted as if they wanted out, especially France where de Gaulle's return to power in May 1958 seemed ominous in light of his prior opposition to any integrationist scheme. And, states that had opted for abstention already acted as if they wanted in—especially Great Britain, whose attempts to form a broader free trade area depended on Germany's adhesion and American support. Denied the former because of the Franco-German *rapprochement* engineered by de Gaulle and Chancellor Adenauer in late 1958, but also without the latter because of the explicit preference shown by the Eisenhower and Kennedy administrations for a Common Market with Britain in it, Britain clearly lost this first round of intra-European debate about economic integration in Europe when the initial wave of tariff cutting took place in January 1959 as scheduled. After that, the march toward the Common Market of the Six proceeded at an ever quicker pace. In early 1965, the ECSC and the Economic Community (as well as the European Atomic Energy Community) were merged into the European Communities (EC), and, by mid-1968, the abolition of all remaining tariffs completed the customs union 18 months ahead of the schedule agreed in Rome.

IV

Yet "Europe" could hardly be reduced to a narrow customs union, whether of the few or of the many: There was a political dimension that had to be defined, too, through a similar, parallel process. Reflecting the exaggerated ambitions of the immediate postwar years, there had been in 1950 an elaborate draft proposal for a European Political Community: Linked to the EDC, it died with it in 1954. In the early 1960s, a new proposal, called the Fouchet Plan, outlined a "Union of the States" that was expected to add to the economic community a whole new dimension of consultation and joint action in the area of foreign policy. That proposal, too, failed, following the revisions, exceedingly self-serving, sought by de Gaulle "because our partners, as a whole, did not consider that Europe could exist by itself and deal with questions of policy and defense outside NATO." Combined with other aspects of French policy in the 1960s—including opposition to Britain's entry in the Common Market, withdrawal from NATO, and an offensive against the privileged status of the U.S. dollar the failure of the Fouchet Plan placed the institutional deepening of "Europe" on hold for the balance of the decade.

That the European process was now stalled could be seen perhaps most convincingly on the monetary front, where a proposal for union in 10 years had been endorsed in 1970, with a leading assist from French President Pompidou who made it the centerpiece of the *relance européenne* he sought in coordination with the Federal Republic. Recurring currency crises between 1967 and 1969 followed years of unusual stability and pointed to the diminishing confidence of the international money markets in the entire structure of exchange rates (unusually stable between 1949 and 1967, with the most notable exceptions of two devaluations of the French franc in 1957 and 1958). It was, in part, to gain Bonn's support that Pompidou lifted the French opposition to the admission of Great Britain in the Common Market. As contemplated in the agreement reached at the Hague in December 1969 and as explicitly written in the Werner Plan, an Economic and Monetary Union would help Europe weaken the undue dependence of the member countries on the U.S. dollar at a time when the U.S. payments deficit was rising at an unprecedented pace:

from $9.8 billion in 1970 to $29.8 billion in 1971.[11]

The failure of the Werner Plan and that of the more modest European "snake" that was initially designed to narrow the intra-European currency fluctuations within the American "tunnel" of wider bands permitted by the Smithsonian agreement in 1971, left "Europe" astray amidst apparently irreconcilable intra-European conflicts of economic interests (especially between inflation-prone France and inflation-shy Germany) and political aspirations (on the eve of Britain's entry in the Common Market). Increasingly wary of French policies, German authorities warned against their partners' reliance on German subsidies for the Common Agricultural Policy—"that white elephant," as then Finance Minister Helmut Schmidt called it—and for regional aid, made costly by the dismantlement of the French empire. And, indeed, the *sauve-qui-peut* that characterized the reactions of Western Europe to the 1973 oil embargo appeared to reflect the end of "Europe" as an idea that had apparently run out of time and the submission of Europe as a continent that had literally run out of gas.

The decline of "Europe" seemed all the more irreversible as Britain's entry to the Community in January 1973 plunged "Europe" into endless quarrels at a time of new global challenges that no one European country seemed able to address alone: the ascendancy of Japan's economic power combined with the emergence of other new industrial competitors in Asia, the rise of Soviet military power and ambitions combined with an apparent devaluation of American power and will, and growing instabilities in the Third World, where Europe's vital dependence for raw materials and markets caused further tension with the United States. At the 1978 European

---

11. In fact, European confidence in the theretofore sacrosanct dollar had been jolted 10 years earlier at the time of the dollar "crisis" of October 1960: From that point on, its rate would be continuously scrutinized in the light of the performance, real or perceived, of the American economy. See Charles A. Coombs, *The Arena of International Finance* (New York: John Wiley & Sons, 1976), 57.

summits held in Copenhagen and Bremen, the drive for monetary cooperation was resumed, therefore, by the French president (Giscard d'Estaing) and the German chancellor (Helmut Schmidt). Together, they led the nine EC states to agree to, and join, a new European Monetary System (EMS) that became operational in March 1979 without the inflated rhetoric that had accompanied similar efforts 10 years earlier.

At first, prospects for the EMS looked no better than the stillborn Werner Plan. With a new wave of Europessimism sweeping across the Atlantic, more attention was placed on Britain's refusal to participate in the exchange rate mechanism (which was critical to the new arrangement) than on the system proper. Nor, for that matter, did the EMS do much to alleviate charges of overall irrelevance. Between 1979 and 1984, high and highly different rates of inflation and budget deficits caused frequent and difficult currency realignments among EMS members, who also ignored the currency unit that, as a fixed basket of European currencies (the ECU), was expected to be a vital feature for the effective functioning of the new system.

Notwithstanding this difficult start, the EMS endured surprisingly well the turbulent international monetary markets that accompanied the fall of the dollar after its February 1985 high. The volatility of both nominal and real exchange rates among EMS members declined sharply (with no adjustment from January 1987 to January 1990) and, though the evidence remains tentative, wider exchange-rate relationships too. With the deutsche mark acting as an anchor against inflation—to which high-inflation countries rallied as a demonstration of their conversion to a "rigor" that was especially evident in France after the removal of Prime Minister Pierre Mauroy in early 1983—the EMS afforded its members the opportunity to pursue counter-inflationary policies: As they did so successfully, inflation differentials within the EMS were significantly reduced. The resulting credibility of intra-EMS bilateral exchange-rate stability satisfied a major German objective, namely, to protect its competitiveness in Europe against the fluctuations of the dollar—because the EMS served to moderate the impact of a rise or decline of the U.S. currency against the German currency on the related decline or rise of the deutsche mark against other European currencies. Thus, as Germany's trade surplus with the United States fell from DM28 billion in 1986 to DM17 billion ($9 billion) in 1988, its surplus with other EMS members rose from DM30 billion to DM46 billion, almost eight times the 1983 figure. And the EC share of the Federal Republic's global trade surplus rose from 53.8 percent for the first quarter 1987 to 65.9 percent for the corresponding period in 1988.[12]

This performance proved to be painful for many of the member states, of course: In a monetary system disciplined by the *Bundesbank*, inflation fell more and faster, but unemployment rose higher and longer than in most other industrial countries, thereby necessitating a politically difficult reordering of domestic priorities—especially for the socialist majorities in southern Europe. By 1988, unemployment had returned to its pre-1973 levels in 8 of the 10 OECD countries that were non-EC members (including 5 in Europe). But in all 10 EC countries, unemployment remained close to its peak rate. Yet, later in the decade, overall economic gains proved sufficiently compelling to encourage the charter members to seek new initiatives toward full monetary union among them.

V

The same collegial discipline could not be found in the political arena, where the process of European Political Consultation (EPC) that was launched after the report of the Davignon Committee in October 1970 remained slow and uneven. At the Hague in December 1969, the EC member states accepted President Pompidou's explicit distinction between economic

---

12. See M.J. Artis, "External Aspects of the European Monetary System," in D.E. Fair and C. de Boissieu, eds., *International Monetary and Financial Integration—The European Dimension* (Boston: Kluwer Academic Publishers, 1988), 209-218.

integration, formally embodied in the Rome Treaty, and political consultation, which relinquished final authority to the national governments. In the French view, this distinction appeared to end the quarrel over supranationality: The coordination of foreign policies was to be, and was, left to an informal consultative network that lacked institutional incentives to force adherence to any agreed common policy. If anything, references to "Europe" served as a convenient justification for doing nothing or offending no one—by explaining inaction or diluting action within the self-serving reference to the need for European solidarity. Viewed in this manner, "Europe" was more effective as a convenient shelter from U.S. leadership and its policies than as a responsible agent in periods of crises. In the 1970s, such a pattern proved especially visible with regard to regional crises, from the 1973 War in the Middle East (and the first oil crisis) to the downfall of the Shah in Iran in 1979 (and the second oil crisis) and the Soviet invasion of Afghanistan.

In the 1980s, however, the reflex of collegiality and coordination developed during the previous years began to show a more constructive tone and, on occasion, a more substantive form too. That such would be the case had more to do with an improvement in Atlantic relations than with the actual improvement of the foreign policy collective machinery of "Europe." Deploring America's unilateralism, bemoaning its actions (or inaction), and equating intra-European unity with Atlantic discord faded, in part thanks to the Reagan administration's refusal to turn every one of its policies in the Third World into a test of Atlantic cohesion elsewhere.

Accordingly, first over East-West issues, and next on North-South issues, intra-European and Atlantic differences narrowed: With the French assist on the deployment of U.S. intermediate-range nuclear forces in the Federal Republic prior to the 1983 Williamsburg summit, which was conducive to the most impressive display of intra-European and Atlantic cohesion seen in two decades, and with the coordination of U.S. and European action in the Gulf during the latter stage of the war between

Iran and Iraq—when the Reagan administration succeeded in gaining support from five of the seven members of the Western European Union in clearing mines from the Persian Gulf. For these two examples that involved vital interests for both Europe and the United States, the lesson was the same: The convergence of interests among the members of the European Community, and between the Community and the United States, was translated into a convergence of their policies too. In a real sense, the quick reaction shown by "Europe" to the revolutions of 1989 and the rapid approval given by the Bush administration to the Community's involvement in the reconstruction of Eastern Europe and the construction of a new security system for the Continent, were the logical outcome of such a 20-year-old trend toward the accommodation of intra-European differences.

As could have been expected, when the member states moved closer toward the integration of their economies and the harmonization of their policies, the structures created by the Rome Treaty were increasingly tested. In 1979, the first election of a European Parliament by direct universal suffrage was designed to broaden and deepen public awareness of "Europe" by creating a whole new category of cross-border voters. That this initiative, too, would have been received initially with indifference and skepticism should come as no surprise. Like the Council of Europe 30 years before, the Parliament seemed condemned to inconsequential meetings—a symbolic gesture of goodwill on the part of European governments whose sovereignty could not be challenged by the European Council. Yet, it was Parliament that gave birth to the draft treaty for a European Union that served as a catalyst for the intergovernmental conference that drafted the Single European Act (SEA).

The Union that was envisaged in Parliament ominously dared return to the vision of a "Europe" of the few that left reticent states out, as had been done in 1949 when the Coal and Steel Community was limited to only six of the members of the Council of Europe and in 1958 when the Rome Treaty proceeded without the seven OEEC states that chose to form a free trade association instead. Coming as it did a few weeks before the 1984 European elections, Mitterrand's support for the "basic premise" of the Parliament's draft treaty—a new distribution of power between the Council, the Commission, and the Parliament—aimed at improving an electoral image tarnished by the failure of his policies in 1981–1983.

The French attitude was surprising: A few years earlier, Mitterrand's predecessor had emphasized that Parliament's powers "must be exercised strictly within the terms of the [existing Rome] treaties." And following five years of bitter quarrels and wrecked summit meetings about budget issues, which had brought the European Commission to its lowest ebb, French support for an intergovernmental conference held in order to negotiate a new round of institutional reforms put additional pressures on Britain to settle at last on most of the outstanding budget issues (to avoid exclusion from these new negotiations) and forced Thatcher's hand over a question— that of a single economic market—which she seemed to take lightly anyway.[13]

VI

Even before the revolutions of 1989 carried Europe past the Cold War and its related dislocations, "Europe" was, therefore, well on its way. Clearly, the path toward 1992 had been opened by the transformations of the previous decades. Prompting this new *relance* was the need to attend to the declining competitiveness of the states of Europe in the economic sectors with strongest world growth. The first challenge of the Single European Act (SEA) and its program for a

---

13. "At the time, I wondered whether the British Prime Minister had been advised of the fact that the calling of such a conference was a matter of simple majority. She simulated surprise very successfully if she did in fact know about this procedure." Garrett Fitzgerald (who was Ireland's prime minister at the time of the conference), "1992 and European Economic Unity," *L.S.E. Quarterly* (Autumn 1989), 194.

single market was, therefore, less a challenge to the world without than one imposed by the latter on the Community.[14] In short, 1992 acted as a catalyst for giving Europe the will and the means to contain its decline and restore its competitiveness by attending to a legacy of underinvestment, corporate balkanization, and market fragmentation. Increasingly buoyed by sustained growth, diminishing inflation, and unprecedented corporate earnings (predictably a good indicator of corporate confidence), European industrialists encouraged their governments to build the single market that would permit the benefits of scale economies, while they themselves engaged in various modes of corporate restructuring designed to facilitate the rise of pan-European conglomerates able to compete effectively with their American and Asian rivals in the European and world markets.

Nor was this all, of course. A single economic market *à l 'américaine* could hardly endure and prosper with fragmented political institutions *à l 'européenne*. The inner logic of the Single European Act was, therefore, that of a qualitative leap toward new institutions that would aim at full economic union and even, in a manner left admittedly ambiguous, political union. In mid-1989, the Delors Report on monetary union articulated this logic most explicitly: new or strengthened central European institutions that can manage irrevocably fixed exchange rates, a single currency (primarily for political and psychological reasons), a European system of central banks

---

14. Indeed, the decade that preceded the adoption of the Single European Act had left European exporters with diminishing shares in global trade, especially in the potentially decisive sectors of high technology. Although some of these losses could be dismissed on such grounds as location—particularly in the growing markets of Asia—they were often viewed as a symptom of the declining international competitiveness of European export industries, including those in the Federal Republic (though admittedly to a smaller degree than its European partners). Rolf J. Langhammer and Ulrich Hiemenz, "Declining Competitiveness of EC Suppliers in ASEAN Markets: Singular Case or Symptom?" *Journal of Common Market Studies*, December 1985, pp. 105-119.

"explicitly committed to price stability" (comparable to the Federal Reserve System in the United States, and consisting of an independent EuroFed above the existing national central banks), and macroeconomic policy coordination (which, however, would not impose binding limits on the budget deficits of EC members). A scheme of this sort, complained then-Chancellor to the Exchequer Nigel Lawson in January 1989, "implies nothing less than European government—albeit a federal one—and political union: the United States of Europe." Lawson was prescient: Political union was placed formally on the political agenda by President Mitterrand and Chancellor Kohl in April 1990.

Thus started amidst the ruins inherited from two world wars and tolerated differently and at a different pace by nation states anxious to preserve their fragile autonomy and remaining identity, the long journey toward European integration has continued throughout the years. No grand design met its objectives as each member state always resisted any new erosion of its sovereignty and, predictably, sought ways to pass on to others the internal pains demanded by every new scheme. Yet every failure carried with it the seeds of the marginal progress that followed: Thus reviewed within the broad framework of the past 40 years, the cumulative results of the process suggest that, granted the time they need, the countries of Europe can overcome their divisions and construct a common future, escaping the gloomy predictions that have accompanied their slow but steady progress toward unity.

When that process is ended at last, future historians will claim perhaps that the countries of Europe—"each with its own spirit, its own history, its own language, its own misfortunes, glories, and ambitions"—built "Europe" in a fit of absent-mindedness. There will be much truth to this judgment. Yet, launched in the absence of any explicit definition of—and commitment to—its ultimate objective, this process has shaped nonetheless the emergence of a Community that provides an effective framework within which the old realities of a fragmented past can be addressed with the new thinking of a unified future.

VII

After the Cold War, the future of "Europe" remains tied to the one unthinkable outcome envisioned throughout the years: the end of Germany's division, out of which grow the promise—Germany in "Europe"—and the fear—Europe in Germany—evoked by the dominance of German economic power on the Continent.

Predicated on the permanence of German division, postwar schemes for Europe were not especially popular in Germany, where they were perceived as a galling infringement of German sovereignty. Beyond widespread suspicion of French motives, the reasons for such opposition were many. In the case of the Schuman Plan, Kurt Schumacher and his Social Democratic Party (SPD) feared that Britain's refusal to join the proposed Community might cut off Germany from progressive northern Europe and lead it into a small Europe where Christian Democratic majorities would effectively prevent the socialization of the German economy. In the case of the Pleven Plan, Schumacher and the SPD quickly saw rearmament—widely opposed at the time—as a route to gain power in the scheduled elections of 1953 or before. Rearmament, they complained, was designed to absorb the Federal Republic into a political ensemble *à la française* ("Europe") and a military alliance *à l'américaine* (NATO), as if there were no other Germany. As a result of such political obstruction and military designs, any prospect of reunification would have to be abandoned, and Germany's division would be made permanent without achieving either security or even stability for its Western half. For, according to Adenauer's critics, the Chancellor's "collaboration with the occupation" was predicated on his offer of Germany's territory as both the battlefield of retreat and the battlefield of liberation, thereby condemning the German people to being the mass casualties of a "double scorched-earth policy" imposed upon them by the armies of the East and of the West.

Even in those early postwar years, nationalism was the key

to Germany's own political debate about its future. Although the moral and aesthetic example set by Schumacher in resisting Hitler gave him an unchallenged grip on his party until his death in August 1952, the bitterness of his personality, the aggressive edge of his rhetoric, and his unrelenting emphasis on Germany's reunification, compounded Western anxieties. There was a man, wrote Dean Acheson of Schumacher, who "combined a harsh and violent nature with nationalist and aggressive ideas." Compared to him, Konrad Adenauer—whose Christian Democratic party barely edged the SPD in the 1949 elections and whose election as chancellor had been decided by one vote (his own) in the German *Bundestag*—was indeed "our" man in Bonn.[15]

Adenauer's reaction to the Soviet proposals of March 1952, setting forth the conditions of reunification (including neutrality and disarmament) and a general peace treaty, precluded serious debate about Germany's reunification for the next three-and-a-half decades. For Adenauer, even a united Germany could not remain both neutral *and* independent for long in the face of the continuing threat that would be raised by the Soviet Union. If it was disarmed, who would keep it independent? If it was armed, who would keep it neutral? Rather than pursue the elusive shadow of negotiations with the East, which offered the tantalizing hope of unity, Adenauer preferred the more tangible substance of an immediate integration of the FRG in an Atlantic community that guaranteed security and in a European community that restored national legitimacy.

---

15. "There was a man," thought Acheson after his first meeting with Adenauer, "whose mind could travel the road along which all our measures for the recovery and security of Europe had been moving." *Sketches from Life of Men I Have Known* (New York: Harper, 1959), 171. About Schumacher (whom Acheson met only once), the secretary of state later wrote: "When death relieved the Social Democrats of Schumacher's leadership, the party rapidly resumed a constructive role in German political life." *Present at the Creation* (New York: W.W. Norton, 1969), 361-362.

But because he found the long-term stability and identity of the German state threatened by Adenauer's abandonment of the goal of unity, Schumacher insisted on preserving a negotiating option that would, at the very least, postpone any interim action that might provoke either party into leaving the table. The issue was not rearmament, which Schumacher did not reject as a matter of principle, and even less pacifism, which Schumacher did reject as a matter of principle, but reunification, without which there could be neither security nor stability.

Neither Schumacher nor his immediate successor at the helm of the SPD, Erich Ollehauer, appeared ready to acknowledge that none of the other powers in and out of Europe would support reunification in practice. In the West, the kind of reunited Germany envisaged by the SPD could become all too easily a weak neutral state opened to influence from the East or a strong and domineering third force oblivious to Western influence—which, in either case, was much less in the interest of the West than the existing status quo. In the East, the kind of reunited Germany envisaged by the CDU could become just as easily a strong *revanchiste* state aligned with the West, which was much less in the Soviet interest than Germany's continued division. Even the half-hearted negotiations over the Eden plan offered by the Western powers in January 1954 were hardly more than a disingenuous attempt by both sides to preserve the status quo: against the Soviet bait of a reunited but disarmed and neutral Germany and against the American offer of a divided but rearmed and aligned Germany.

In any case, after the enlargement of NATO and the establishment of the Warsaw Pact in May 1955, little room was left for compromise, even of an illusory nature. Henceforth, the Soviets insisted, the issue would be an internal matter that would have to be negotiated directly between the two German governments in Bonn and Pankow. From that point on, as long as Moscow held the power needed to ensure that the regime in Pankow got the terms it sought, reunification was no longer an issue. Whether through bilateral negotiation or mutual indifference, the East German state would survive. This being the case, the SPD no longer had a viable or particularly relevant foreign policy: Indeed, many of the SPD's early opponents of rearmament—including Willy Brandt and a young Helmut Schmidt—lost no time in becoming the most determined supporters of the *Bundeswehr* and NATO. But given the growing prosperity achieved by the CDU policies—which amounted to Ludwig Erhard's so-called economic miracle—the SPD no longer had an electorally viable economic policy either, thereby setting the stage for the party's agonizing reappraisal at Bad Godesberg.

Thus, what foreclosed Germany's internal debate about reunification—and, accordingly, about membership in NATO and the EEC—had to do with both the perceived reliability of the American commitment and the reliable credibility of Soviet hostility. Although there were many challenges to both assumptions throughout the years—repeatedly in the West, occasionally in the East—the German Democratic Republic's illusion of national legitimacy died a sudden death in the streets in 1989, and the illusion of allied restraints on the resulting drive for German unification died in the ballot box the following year.

VIII

Defining a Europe that is free from U.S. tutelage and Soviet influence is hardly a novel objective. What is new, however, is that, now, the countries in the East, including the USSR, are feared more for what they might become (an economic and political burden) than for what they used to be (a military and political threat). Accordingly, in contrast with the exuberance shown during previous phases of détente, Europe's rhetoric on behalf of change remains moderate and even apprehensive.

Thus, Soviet calls for a "common European house" are heard skeptically, whether in European capitals or in Brussels. There is no more than a "European village," explains Jacques

Delors, where the "house" explicitly owned by the Community is separate from other dwellings built by other European countries or leased by non-European states (including the United States and the associated states of Asia and the Third World). In theory, every effort will be made to end these divisions and form a more comprehensive European space. To do otherwise, as the French president has said, would be an "historic error worse than Yalta." But there remain, in practice, some hesitations—even some reluctance—as if somehow the time was not ripe, the objective not clear, the means not available, the opportunity not promising.

Where else is an explanation to this ambivalence to be found than about the unfinished status of "Europe"? Promises engendered by the new thinking that prevails in the West, as well as in the East, clash with the threats raised by the same old realities of the past, in the East as well as in the West, too: how to end the divisions of the Cold War without returning to the divisions that have harmed the whole history of Europe. "Everything that brings Europeans closer together," Foreign Minister Hans Dietrich Genscher has repeated throughout the years, "does the same for the Germans." With the pace of the latter accelerated dramatically, the French seek anxiously a European Community whose institutions will have been sufficiently strengthened to withstand the weight of German pressures and dilute the autonomy of the German state. "Let us unite Europe," Prime Minister Macmillan allegedly offered de Gaulle in late 1962. "We are three men who can do it together: you, me, and Adenauer."[16] Without the *ménage à trois* that has been often envisioned, but never achieved before, "Europe" will face many more setbacks, which Germany's new status makes more disruptive and perhaps even more dangerous than ever before.

Yet, as the Community provides a framework within which an orderly transformation of the established order in Europe

---

16. Charles de Gaulle, *Mémoires d'espoir: Le renouveau, 1958-1962* (Paris: Plon, 1970), 231.

can take place, politically in the West and economically in the East, the two superpowers cannot be limited to the role of spectators in completing a tale they were so very instrumental in writing 45 years ago. For each of them separately, and both of them jointly, provide the security framework within which any intra-European accommodation is not left to the goodwill of either of the two superpowers or any one of the European countries.

Thus, with the benefit of hindsight for some, and without it for others, a review of the many *relances européennes* of the past confirms the reality of a European presence whose room for maneuver is enlarged by both the promises and the threats of a new political and security order on the European continent. Acting as a magnet that the countries of Eastern Europe find irresistible, the European Community is a pivotal element of the Western strategy toward the East. Even as persisting conflicts among the EC states strengthen or weaken its institutions, the Community is the ultimate moderator of a political dialogue between the two sides of Europe. It provides an effective method for addressing common objectives whose fulfillment will contribute ultimately to the emergence of Europe's new realities, including the reality of a dominant and unified German state.

This political dialogue among Europeans overlaps with a military dialogue between the two superpowers. One deals directly with the new boundaries of permissible change; the other deals directly with the new boundaries of mutual security. Both dialogues feed on each other: The tone, the substance, and the results observed in one affect the tone, the substance, and the results of the other. At some point in the future, of course, both dialogues will merge into an inseparable whole. But that point has not been reached yet: There are still many tales to be told, questions to be answered, plots to be revealed in the saga of European integration, German unification, and superpower accommodation. For all of these, the conclusion appears unquestionable—namely, the end of the many divisions that have been the cause and the result of the various postwar conflicts. And even though the commitment to taking and coordinating the steps required for the continued and stable fulfillment of this purpose remains still in doubt, "Europe" already stands midway between the fragmented normalcy of interstate relations and the integrated normalcy of intrastate relations.

VI

Between East and West: East-Central Europe's Future Past

George Liska

T HE SOVIET REVOLUTION from above and its by-product in the East-Central European revolutions from below have set off aftershocks that may yet convulse international relations in ways that overturn the contemporary predominance of economic issues, without subsuming history, and its perennial conflicts in a transcendent utopia.

Widest in scope and most immediate in impact, but also shallowest in long-term significance, are the pressures unleashed by these revolutions for a reversal of alliances that would replicate the diplomatic revolution of the mid-eighteenth century, when France and Austria set aside their longstanding rivalries to constrain to mutual advantage the British and Prussian upstarts. The combination of parallel pressure and constructive example heralds the need for the two former superpowers to cling together lest they be cashiered separately by the real victors of the Cold War—Germany and Japan.

Less immediate, but more significant, is the growing appeal of a return to the modes of organizing political space that preceded the triumph of the modern territorial state. At issue once again, as a result of the eclipse of "the state" as idea and value, is the possibility of reviving in updated form the medieval pluralist pattern of graduated authority. In a context that reaches beyond the whole of Europe, such an

This essay is an excerpt from a cycle of lectures delivered in May 1990 at the Charles University in Prague. *Falling Dominions, Reviving Powers: Germany and Europe's Unfinished Agenda in the East* will be published by The Johns Hopkins Foreign Policy Institute in the late fall of 1990.

order in East-Central Europe might serve to dissipate a conflict much older and more ardent than the Cold War ever was.

The two reversals—of alliances and of political orders—are interdependent; upon their mutual success rest the best prospects for rebuilding structures of stability to replace the *disjecta membra* of the waning security systems, first of all in Europe.

II

What are the implications of this new state of things? Who are the principal European players?

First, France. France is entitled to style itself the *grande nation* because it was the model for the European kind of statehood in all the phases of its evolution. France is, for the same reason, the indispensable fountainhead of legitimation for any kind of future order, acting from its present relative weakness just as it had acted earlier on the basis of growing strength. Yet now, just as during the two past centuries, France will also continue to experiment with ways and means to confront the consequences of its gradual weakening in relation to the Germanic neighbor, currently inside the European Community. Final decline caught up with France after it had been lowered from the peak of its primacy by its still-longer-lasting English rival. This means that French diplomacy will be always tempted to seek an empowering relationship with East European states and will only reluctantly undergo alliance ties that, dominated by America today just as previously by England, after issuing out of power-political debility, enfeeble it psychologically.

Second, Great Britain. Great Britain will continue to waver between a European future and an Atlantic past at a time when it can no longer exploit either political divisions on the Continent nor material advantages gained from leadership in Europe's industrial revolution. Once the struggles between powers of the land and the sea had raised England to overseas supremacy and to unavowed hegemony on the Continent, the growing cost of the struggle with France and the finally ruinous confrontation with Germany forced proud Albion onto its knees before the centerpiece of its first empire, in the so-called special relationship. The more demeaning this reversal proves to be in present circumstances, the more will England resist finding itself as it was before its rise to global prominence, an extracontinental island, insignificant strategically and culturally isolated. Unneeded by a self-sufficient Europe, it would be undesired by its one-time colony so long as the global balance of power of immediate interest to the United States was not at risk. Such an England will continue to complement France in withstanding, with perturbing consequences, the fate that sooner or later overtakes all great powers.

Third, Germany. Following the fiasco of the Weimar Republic and its Nazi *sequelae*, the Federal Republic gives rise anew to problems that the Wilhelmine Reich was the latest to instigate in conditions of relative peace and stability. As the successor to the imperial entity assembled around Prussia, with its center now shifted westward, a united Germany will be again under an obligation to clarify its true personality for itself and for others and define its true vocation outside a but provisionally serviceable North Atlantic framework. By virtue of its economic strength, Bonn today, and Berlin tomorrow, will be a source of problems that can be only superficially distinguished from predicaments spawned by its predecessors in economically more precarious settings.

All great states dispose of but a finite range of historically rooted orientations, variable mainly as to the ways of adapting them to contemporary power relationships and organizational instruments. Thus, France was able to choose between the West European option of some association with the Rhenish part of Germany, the East European option of alliance with first Scandinavian and subsequently Slavic states, and, as the last recourse, the Atlantic one of accommodation with the day's Anglo-Saxon power. In Germany's case, a conservative orientation would carry on Bismarck's primary concern to stabilize the gains from the first unification (1871). For Bonn to maintain evenhanded relations with both of the flanking powers, Soviet in lieu of tsarist Russia and the United States in lieu of England, would be the opposite of seeking additional concrete gains at either's cost by playing off one against the other. In one way or another disruptive were by contrast from the very beginning the policies of the two later chancellors, von Caprivi and von Bülow. Immediately adaptable is the former's policy of the "new course," shaping a complex of trade treaties into a politico-economic *Mitteleuropa* under the cover of amicable relations with the dominant sea power (Great Britain then, the United States today) and of overtly not inimical relations with the Eastern continental neighbor (still Russia). The policy was expected to reach only gradually, and without risk of war, the goals that Bülow later enlarged overseas and radicalized in Europe. After Caprivi's commercially implemented Western-liberal alternative had failed to bring forth the anticipated results, a policy of the free hand between the wing powers was expected to guarantee decisive concrete gains by virtue of an alliance imposed on a Russia that had incurred initial setbacks in the presumptively unavoidable final struggle with the Anglo-Saxon great power.

Fourth, Russia. This Eastern colossus had been again causing panic in the West before, like many times previously, it disclosed its clay feet. The Soviet Union reproduced once again a rhythm from the tsarist past when, barely a day after engaging in regional repression, it incurred regime decay of its own, and when, having redressed in the depths of its vast space the power balance between more Western states, most recently against Hitlerite Germany, it is again being shown the way out of Europe and toward Asia.

Fifth, the smaller states taking up the space, if not the role, of either the Ottoman or the Habsburg empire. They are once more precariously situated between the possibility of improving on their fate or reenacting it, more as the victims than instigators of Europe's ills before and between the world wars. Many of them will again look back nostalgically to the Habsburg conglomerate, forgetting that once the Austro-Hungarian empire had fulfilled its mission vis-à-vis the Turkish East, it proved unable to fit the Slavs into its structure on an equal basis with the Magyars and was, as a result, unable to withstand the attractive force of the Germanic North. Adding aggression to the attraction was subsequently enough to terminate the area's small-state experiment with an ease and brutality that was equalled only by the Third Reich's Left-totalitarian successors. In a longer view of things, both totalitarian orders were also the products of failed liberal-nationalist efforts to found formal independence in materially inadequate and strategically insecure lodgings.

Nazi violence was but one element in a deeper and wider-ranging interwar pathology. For this reason alone, the Third Reich illumined, however luridly, a pathway toward lasting future recovery. Integrating the material and human resources of Western Europe in the Nazi war machine provided a model for the supranational integration Jean Monnet was to preach and later assist in realizing. Less obvious is the possibility that Hitler's evoking the position of Bohemia and Moravia within the orbit of the medieval Germanic empire as a formal warrant for the so-called Protectorate signaled not only a first step toward consolidating further and vaster gains in the decisive phase of the Anglo-German era of continental-maritime contentions, but also intimated something else: a possible solution for East-Central Europe in the Cold War's aftermath, a solution that might help prevent the recently interrupted worldwide contention from being resumed in the future.

III

The situation in East-Central Europe is not uniform, even in the critical northern sector between Germany and Russia that comprises Poland and Czechoslovakia. The challenges confronting the latter state may, however, be considered representative of basic problems.

Present possibilities for Czechoslovakia's future are delimited by temporal and spatial factors that converge on the conditions of effective state building. Whereas the temporal factor directs vision to an ever-receding past, the spatial given points to re-extending the relevant west-to-east geographic axis globally.

The least remote past is condensed in the beginnings and the life experiences of the Czechoslovak republic issuing from World War I. That republic embodied the optimistic liberal-nationalistic spirit of the era and stood as such for an attempt to forge a seemingly easy, because substantively but mechanical, link to the West. A sentimentally propagandized alliance with France seemed to represent a shortcut to the terminus of an emotive journey. When the Munich awakening forced the effort to redirect the linkage to the Soviet east, this proved to be as premature in its presuppositions (that is, Stalinism democratized by the war experience) as had been the interwar connection. Starting at the latest in the late 1960s, the pro-Western bias reasserted itself fully as a reaction to disillusionment with an equally abortive, international-proletarian in lieu of national-liberal and, in reality, totalitarian shortcut supposed to lead to a statehood as humane and socially satisfying as it was secure. Today's pro-Westernism has assumed the guise of enthusiasm for an institutionally secured supranational European unity within the framework of the greatest possible detachment from the East. As such, it is the generic equivalent of membership in the Franco-English system of collective security, a mere facade in the pretended security structure against a vanquished (but internally strengthened) Germany, which was the object of the Czechoslovak leadership's hopes in the years after 1918.

A longer regression into a more remote era recalls an essentially Central European organization in the form of the Habsburg monarchy. Initially legitimated as a defense barrier against the (then Ottoman) East, that kind of order could be revived less in close association with a Poland that outgrew the parts falling to the Habsburgs under the eighteenth century partitions than with a Hungary that shrank from its Slavs-comprising dominion of the Crown of St. Stephen under the Austro-Hungarian Compromise of 1876, as well as with now-neutral Austria and past it toward the Adriatic south (once the empire's Lombardy-Venetia). Close ties of this kind are then supposed to insulate the small-state bloc sufficiently from an ostensibly weakened present East and serve as either a passageway or antechamber to a seemingly triumphant West.

The Habsburg era is a historical epoch and order that, more even than the interwar conditions, evokes the many-sided character of the relationship between Slav and German. Austria-Hungary demonstrated the attendant cluster of problems within a constitutional-juridical framework that did not polarize the relationship to quite the degree a liberal-national Czechoslovak state ultimately did, but the monarchy for all that did not create a successful inter-ethnic framework capable of appeasing the dissension by equalizing the relationship.

Within a perspective that is, one way or another, unpromising, where can be found even but symbolic signs and even but only gradually realizable patterns for a German-Slav coexistence that would be equal in principle and equalizable in practice? Is it necessary to continue the journey in time all the way to the medieval antecedents of the Habsburg empire? It is in fact useful to search there for analogies pertinent for the present, and it might be possible to find them in the era's many-sided and multidirectional feudal engagements and vertically graduated central and local jurisdictions. What might emerge out of the search would then be a modern version of inter- and intrastate pluralism better suited to put the Slavic-Germanic relationship on a more solid and enduring foundation in Central and Eastern Europe than had proved possible for the devices of either so-called Austro-Slavism within, or a pan-Slavism largely outside, the Habsburg imperial system—or for ethnic nationalism within the succeeding republican framework.

IV

As regards the all-important larger setting, it will remain still for a time, however conditionally, shaped by the state of U.S.-Soviet relations. Their condition reflects two factors, one of which is organic and the other strategic. The organic factor consists of a mutual enfeeblement that has climaxed in the notorious Soviet crisis and in an only less visibly manifest American decline. The United States has unavoidably weakened not only in relation to its immediate postwar condition, but has weakened also relative to the resources it needs for retaining a leading role in the forthcoming general reorganization. The fact that the Soviet crisis is more easily diagnosed means that it can be more precisely analyzed and can, therefore, be cured in principle, even if not as assuredly in fact. The current crisis reenacts a chronic, but recurrently repairable, fragility typical for all militarily constituted continental East, including the East European great powers. In all relevant respects, the converse has traditionally been the gradual and, toward the end, accelerating weakening of national economies based on linear transoceanic ties, once they had reached their evolutionary apex within a nonrepeatable cycle of rise and decline.

The relative American weakening exhibits all of the customary symptoms of gradual eclipse, including the nonmaterial ones. In the conditions of post-industrial economics, such symptoms do not unavoidably bespeak irreversibly unfavorable tendencies within basic structures. However, it is critical for strategic purposes that the three main instrumental pillars that propped up America's postwar foreign policy have been losing their efficacy and forfeiting their utility. The substance of the first, the military-technology pillar, was the so-called strategic triad of land-, sea-, and air-based legs of nuclear deterrence. The triad has become less useful as the sense of Soviet threat, one attendant on a statically bipolar tension, has weakened in favor of more elastic multilateral relationships. Yet, simultaneously with it has weakened also the traditionally central, and henceforth newly important, economic and financial weapon of the

United States. With its waning has disappeared the capacity to dominate global institutions for economic development in the Third World, and the odds for keeping alive the North Atlantic defense organization and broadening America's role inside European institutions have worsened. Changes of this kind have underlined a deficiency previously covered up by the bias favoring the concrete instrumentalities—to wit, a certain lack of historically perfected diplomatic virtuosity making up for massive pressure in maneuverings among manifold power-wielding centers, each disposing of a range of options.

The direction of U.S. foreign policy has been lately only trying in this connection to catch up with a newly revealed Soviet strategic inventiveness, building on more consistent past cultivation of traditional European diplomatic forms and usages. The effort to revitalize America's diminished usefulness in Europe by participation in its economic and security organizations has been the so-far insufficient response to Gorbachevite acrobatics. The purpose of the latter has been to barter power monopoly in an obsolete regional empire for a role in reshaping global equilibrium while coping with a cluster of the kind of problems the United States had in a milder form overcome sequentially: (1) a crisis of national unity endangered by secession, a disruption the Soviets are facing not only in the south, but also in the north; (2) a crisis of the economic system, which a socialistic ingredient implicit in the New Deal had eased for capitalism in the 1930s, while the crisis of Soviet-type socialism has required a markedly larger dose of capitalism; and (3) a crisis of regional hegemony.

In the Western Hemisphere, the United States has been applying the Rooseveltian principle of "good neighborliness" only imperfectly, continuing to claim a veto on extra-hemispheric interference. The late Soviet evacuation of East-Central Europe has been more thorough. If Moscow was guided by the intention of prying reunified Germany out of the exclusive Western embrace, Washington would anchor that same Germany (and root itself) inside Western Europe as a brace against Eastern temptations. Likewise, contrary to the American effort to reconstitute the Western alliance as a political organ, has been the Soviet aim of gradually liquidating NATO as a military alliance. And if the Soviet retreat from East-Central Europe has been a precondition to securing West European assistance in revitalizing the Soviet economy, the hoped-for rehabilitation is one that might in Soviet calculations clear the way to a continent-wide diplomatic primacy resting on the uniquely preserved Russian capacity to act politico-militarily outside Europe in the interest of a wider West. One ultimate aim of Soviet strategy has been to recover equality with the United States in the world at large; the other and, in the last resort, more important goal is long-term defense against China on the Eurasian land mass.

Operational divergences of this nature between the former superpowers complement the organically constituted differences between crisis and decline. Gradually lessening both differences and securing Russian cooperation in international reconstruction does not primarily require extending security guarantees to the Soviets in Europe, but rather necessitates palpable evidence that the United States was not intent on pushing them out of all global positions and assets. Encouraging the Russians' stake in continuing to develop U.S.-Soviet partnership outside Europe is the surest guarantee of their good behavior in Europe—and the other way around.

V

How can the waning specter of a U.S.-Soviet condominium be at least partially revitalized and put to a constructive use? One thing is all the more indisputable because it has been unconditionally corroborated historically. If both rival superpowers have weakened each other to the benefit of third parties, so had Athens and Sparta previously in antiquity, Roman emperors and popes in the Middle Ages, and the Spanish and Ottoman empires at the dawn of the modern era. In time's continuing course the same was sequentially if not simultaneously true for both Holland and Spain as they receded to the advantage of

England, for England only later than for France in favor of Germany, and for the latter just as for Great Britain in favor of its one-time colony. First among the profiteers from the U.S.-Soviet struggle, even before the Federal Republic of Germany, has been Japan and might in the longer term and then dangerously become China: that is to say, one way or another, Asia. The fact that both of the two ostensibly ascendant powers, Japan and Germany, are first of all economically potent expresses a contemporary reversal in the substance of interstate relations that is neither the first of its kind, nor necessarily lasting. And the correspondingly limited range of their potency creates for both Germany and Japan the probability that their ascendancy will do no more than occupy an interregnum between the end of one epoch and the onset of the next.

The predominance of one national economy is even less enduring than the preponderance of the economic factor in international relations ever was. All that cannot be foretold is whether the next turn in favor of politico-militarily strategic instruments and objectives will be the result of worldwide, or only regionally confined, economic crisis that restores the psychological foundations of the state or will be the reaction to a moral crisis precipitated by the uncompensated decline of traditional statehood. No more reliably can one predict the identity of the power reenacting in such a case the performance of the Macedonian who exploited the decline of both Athens and Sparta and of their progressively feebler and less worthy Greek successors. The question would be posed when a Europe united in its present form around Germany or a Franco-German (neo-Carolingian) core proved unfit to realize a historically unprecedented novelty: that is, failed to move beyond the mere simulation of power politics (as all other overmature state systemic segments failed to move), toward reacquiring the capacity for asserting itself effectively in both Eurasian and global space.

The future Macedon might in such an eventuality become a Russia alienated from a restrictively defined and so ineffectual "Europe," or a China that has meanwhile outgrown Russia materially. A United States reoriented toward the Pacific Ocean and a rearmed Japan might then try separately or jointly to mobilize a Europe relegated into the rear-continental posture relative to one or another of the remaining Eurasian great powers. However, the United States would first have to overcome an inner flaw peculiar to insular powers: At all times, such commercial states have been hard put to prolong and never able to recover a "capitalistically" achieved economic leadership once they had reached the apogee of a typically meteoric trajectory. As for Japan, it would in addition have to have found ways economically to penetrate a culturally and demographically superior China or else maintain militarily, on its own, the balance between the Middle Kingdom and the Russia-centered realm.

In neither case would such a scenario place East-Central Europe in a particularly favored position. More promising than a Germano-Japanese interregnum (occupying the time between the triangular insular-continental contentions centered on the Atlantic West and their revival with focus in the Pacific East) is an at least temporary and initially unequal U.S.-Soviet global partnership. Even much weakened, such a partnership would hold the bulk of politically usable military power, even if not the mass of happenings, within a correspondingly enlarged West defined to include European Russia as one of its wing powers.

A closely connected requirement for the West European countries is to release diplomatic and other means for quieting apprehensions that link the present to the times before and between the two world wars. This might mean slowing rather than speeding the growth of a common economic organization, lest it fall apart after having been all too precipitately deepened inside and widened externally. Neither in the guise of an economic (including monetary) union nor as a politicized super-state will the West European complex be capable of diverting reunited Germany from the East for keeps, not by means of ever-increasing material well-being any more than in case of economic difficulties. Even a French diplomacy trying to solve the German question on the Germans' behalf in the direction of French interests will not square the circle by accelerating the 1992 agenda. The sooner France gives up that ambition (and frees Bonn from the obligation to give tactical support), the abler will it be to calm the apprehensions the radical German surge causes by legitimating them without for all that endangering either economic or political cooperation with a Germany that has chosen the conservative route in Europe. And to the same extent that Great Britain has found a place within the extra-European agenda of the modern era's world powers, the more readily will it be able to fill up any gaps in the Russo-American partnership for underpinning world order.

A partnership between yesterday's enemies would realize that which Great Britain often attempted in the past, but made always finally impossible in relations with both pre- and post-revolutionary France and post-Bismarckian Germany. All that would be henceforth needed is for the United States not to recombine British-style indecisiveness and intransigence of the kind that only exacerbated the ambitions of Germany's post-Bismarckian leadership. Like all its continental predecessors, the Soviet Union would accept the limitations implicit in an unequal partnership only if they did not permanently rule out effective equality or parity.

For this reason alone, the implied *renversement des alliances* can only be a pale reflection of the eighteenth-century model of a diplomatic revolution in both manner and purpose, in accord with the contemporary manner of always diluted and often only simulated power politics. Thus modified, the partnership would still be one for collusively entrenching both formerly leading powers in weakened positions for a period sufficient to monitor and if necessary constrain the modus operandi of newly upstart powers. It dramatically confirms the shift of primacy in world politics from operational skill and dynamics to organic substance that the need and opportunity for U.S.-Soviet realignment did not require either extraordinary strategic opportunities or risks in the shadow of an acutely threatening or as a result of a consummated real war. It was sufficient for the reciprocal enfeeblement of the two main adversaries relative to the real third-party winners in a merely "Cold" War to radically modify the values, expand the setting, and affect the perceptions of the main variables in the equation critical for the course and resolution of the historic series of triangularized land-sea power conflicts: the "objective" distance, reflecting disparity, in levels and kinds of economic development between the insular power (lately the United States) and the would-be amphibious continental challenger (lately the Soviet Union) and the latter's "subjective" sense of physically threatening proximity to the rear-continental state (lately China).

As a result, just as the altered conditions have been sufficient to displace the pressures for a cooperative resolution of the conflict from the normative requirement of avoiding a historically mandated terminal military engagement to the more compelling ground of structurally mandated diplomatic expediency, so what might but a short time earlier have amounted to an effective condominium has since been devalued to a mutual insurance compact against sequentially timed, but ultimately parallel, demotion in the world at large, culminating in, if not preceded by, shared exclusion from a meaningful role in Europe. In the process, the superpowers' near-equal superiority in nuclear weapons, after helping avoid armed conflict, but failing to force closer union from strength, has become the key prop of the residual eminence of the two fallen giants, for them to shape into a diplomatic weapon together or taste separately the bitter medicine of the new economics. However, if the operational factor resting on force is to have a role in the interregnum, though one less dramatic than the empowered economic forces, an ostensibly less weakened United States will have to eschew the traditional inhibition to a timely accord between receding ex-enemies. It must withstand the temptation to sacrifice the only hypothetical and long-term benefits of realignment to the immediate tactical advantage of latching onto the once-subordinate third party's rising star.

VI

It is more difficult to identify and implement concrete foundations of order than to derive an ideal scheme of a general system of security. Nothing is easier once inner weaknesses and hidden contradictions have been overlooked. Thus, to keep the North Atlantic alliance in being principally as a safeguard against German revisionism means transforming the alliance from a deterrent against an outside adversary into an irritant among the allies. By the same token, "anchoring" a reunited Germany in the West is expected to block the destabilizing consequences of a neutrality enabling the Germans to play the West off against the East. However, this precaution is in both practical and logical contradiction with the fact that the selfsame waning of East-West polarization that makes transforming NATO from a military into a political organism possible also makes an effective German policy of balancing impracticable.

Equally as dubious is a new pan-European security organization that would replace ideological blocs (the Atlantic and the Warsaw Pacts) and complement Europe's economic with military-political unity. A collective security that comprises all will be unavoidably limited to general commitments to consultation and verification of partial disarmament. Such commitments are in principle compatible with a free hand eastward for the Germans in politico-economic matters. And the commitments' ambiguity might also create an occasion for the kind of tactically all-too-elastic posturing between West and East that is more generally identified with German neutrality. Earlier polarization would then be followed by a different way of tearing Europe asunder or an even more subversive, because unacknowledged, fragmentation.

Military alliances are always directed against someone and only derivatively for something. A security organization will not be successful so long as the identity of the threatening subject (Germany or Russia) is as uncertain as is the object of concern (military or political danger, territorial revisionism, or merely the use of economic strength to revise political relationships).

Equally damaging will be the effort to conceal the real purpose of self-defense or artfully disguise it.

Moreover, an interstate organization of any kind is not sufficient to supplement the members' formal juridical equality with effective parity. An effort to repress power-political and like inequalities will merely exacerbate them. And to the extent that the organization mediates rather than moderates the expression of inequalities, it tends to legitimize them. Its existence puts to sleep apprehensions about the future; insofar as the organization assuages the immediate sense of crisis, it brings the final catastrophe nearer. This was the ultimate effect of the League of Nations and will again be the consequence of similarly conceived European organs of security, in the guise of either "councils" or of "commissions," especially if not supported regionally in the East as firmly as in the West.

The fate of global organizations of collective security, the United Nations following the League of Nations, shows that they can be effective only in conditions in which they are largely superfluous. The same will be true of all-inclusive European organizations. As regards the North Atlantic Alliance, it is supposed to hinder German political expansiveness from West to East and simultaneously deter the militarily still potent Soviets from aggression out of the East westward. Thus, a pan-European organization of security is expected to shield, against different kinds of threats, Europe's West against its East, East against West, and, in yet another way, the East-Central sector against both. This recalls the interwar Locarno Pact, whose impossible task was to protect France against Germany and Germany against France. The fact that commitments and guarantees were then limited to the western boundary of Germany and thus implicitly gave the latter a free hand eastward is currently of interest concerning the capacity of future arrangements to shield that East from politico-economic pressures.

A different possible analogy is with the pre-Locarno German-Soviet understanding arrived at outside, if not against, the West and recorded by history under the name Rapallo. The clandestine military collaboration of the then two international outcasts would be only approximately reproduced by the presence of Soviet troops in the eastern part of a reunited Germany, should the latter offset continuing membership in the Atlantic by acceding to the Warsaw Pact. More pertinent in the long run than that so-far but tentatively ventilated possibility was the potential of any comparable security superstructure to conceal an effective German-Soviet condominium in East-Central Europe as the de facto component or practical consequence of a prominent German participation in the economic reconstruction of the Soviet Union. A neutral bloc of states between Germany and Russia appears to be more advantageous for the countries of East-Central Europe. However, such a bloc would more likely create a power vacuum between democratic Western Europe and either authoritarian or anarchic Eastern Europe than insulate the former from the latter. More than once, including the Ribbentrop-Molotov Pact, has such a vacuum recommended to the larger powers a deal at the expense of the small intervening ones as an alternative to competition momentarily unprofitable for either great power.

If the kernel of real dangers is to be addressed, it is first of all necessary to identify it. One such danger lurks in the decomposition of the tripartite Slavic core of the Soviet Union climaxing peripheral defections. Pushed thus out of Europe and encircled between the Ukrainian-German solidarity of interests and a Chinese irredenta, the Great Russian nation would finally be forced to react to the ensuing isolation militarily along the full conventional-nuclear spectrum. The other real danger consists of Germany drifting into demands for what the diplomatic euphemism calls rectification of East-Central European realities, underscored economically and implemented by political pressures emanating out of inter-party demagogy brought forth by either economic depression or material satiety. One way or another primarily critical, the development and expression of Great Russian nationalism will be both the central factor of European stability and the critical background to any intensification of German nationalism. A liberal reorganization of the Soviet Union can ease pressures on its ethnic core group and make it more likely for the two— moderate Russian nationalism and a liberalized Soviet commonwealth—to serve as a barrier to German expansiveness. Or, alternately, a radicalized Great Russian chauvinism can render a successful Soviet reorganization impossible and, as a reaction to the failure, create conditions that either facilitate the renewal of German drive to the East or render it mandatory.

The surest defense against such future dangers is not a strategy that would once again invert the thrust and direction of an East-Central *cordon sanitaire*, from shielding the Soviets to shutting them out. It is, rather, necessary to convert containment to changed direction and purpose: from limiting Soviet expansionism to confining centrifugal forces from within the Soviet Union. If this is to be done in the interest of the Union's greatest possible voluntary unity, the other and complementary objective must be to limit the scope of an externally targeted expansive potential of united Germany with help from it no less voluntary internal disarticulation. The common institutional denominator is the constitutional principle and practice of confederation. A potentially important Czechoslovak and Polish contribution consists in employing renewed statehood for self-limiting association with thus restructured neighbors.

VII

Suitably formulated, a Czechoslovak and Polish association with the Soviet Union would serve as defense against both dangers—as a political and, in case of need, military-political counterpoise to a politicized expression of German economic supremacy and as a psychopolitical and cultural constraint on, and impediment to, specifically, a west Ukrainian separatism that has traditionally either sought the support or succumbed to the attraction of Germany as the favored counterweight to the Great Russians. Both purposes could be satisfied without the Czech or Czech-Polish commitment being either flagrantly or provocatively targeted at the Bonn Republic in other than narrowly defined conditions that pointed to forcibly pursued territorial or legal-political revisionism. The Warsaw Pact would be thus unostentatiously removed as a device overcome by history, burdened by past misuse (1968), and comprising members (Hungary, Rumania, Bulgaria) who share neither the strategic position nor the vital interests of the northern-tier countries. A simultaneous contractual undertaking to consult the Federal German Republic on the above-mentioned questions would partially offset the more intimate link to Russia, just as a parallel Czechoslovak-Polish consultation relationship with France would further defuse both the pro-Soviet and the anti-German bias of the treaty complex, even if it had not been completed by a promise of mutual nonaggression with Bonn. (Any kind of treaty relationship with France would realize the effort, preceding the Communist coup d'état in February 1948, to broaden a one-sided Czech tie to the Soviet neighbor.)

Mutually complementary undertakings would finally loosen the existing polarization in Europe between the Atlantic and the Warsaw Pacts without dangerously dissolving all associative structures on a continent dislocated into separate fragments around an as much attracting as repelling united Germany.

All interstate engagements that are seriously meant and effectively observed will limit the partners' activities in the interest of a shared purpose. For either or both of the smaller countries to assume a further limitation of sovereignty would be but a supplemental means of pursuing the purposes specific to the international engagements (and would, in addition, be in line with a general tendency). The only precondition is that the self-limitation not be an isolated one, but instead be an integral part of a wider regional arrangement, one aiming at a more than federative, that is, confederal, reorganization of a reunited Germany as much as of a reconsolidated Soviet Union. The shared limitation could in such a setting consist of precisely defined (if initially only a suspensive) competence of interparliamentary Czechoslovak-

(or Czecho-Polish-) German and Soviet commissions on matters of defense and foreign-political and economic issues.

The identity of organs entrusted with these critical competencies determine the specific character of governmental structures. In structures that are only federal, the competencies are reserved for central organs. In *confederal* structures that may be relegated to the upper chambers of legislative bodies (that is, to the *Bundesrat* as against *Bundestag* within the German constitutional tradition), representing individual "states" (the West and East German *Länder*, just as Czech and Slovak or Soviet republics). Only in narrowly circumscribed emergencies could the key competencies be subordinated to the residual jurisdiction of the confederal executive.[1]

Among the several reasons for such an arrangement, one of principle would be to subordinate the foreign policy of both great powers—meaning the foreign-political utilization of German economic and of Soviet military superiority—to the same kind of constraining checks and balances the United States has taken upon itself as part of a different separation of (executive and legislative) powers. The other, inter-nation, part of the arrangement would enable the two smaller states to mediate relations between their great power neighbors. They would function as a link actively rendered impartial by means of the (interparliamentary) procedures implementing the two-sided connection, rather than being formally neutral or statutorily neutralized; as a medium, they would, by the same token, cease to operate as a vacuum of power inciting the Germans and the Soviets into a choice between competition and condominium. More powerful neighbors will unavoidably exert influence. But such influence would be tempered when channeled through formal institutions that made it more responsible

---

1. A strictly cerebral notion in its inception, this line of reasoning was given substance in late May 1990 by the politics surrounding ratification of the State Treaty between West and East Germany, notably as regards the complicating and potentially retarding role of the *Bundesrat* in relation to a too-forward executive.

(and its wielders more accountable) because it would be conspicuously more visible. Because this is commonly insufficient, the influence would be muted further by the institutions being of an intrastate character.

Another, more practical, advantage is this: A voluntarily reshaped Czechoslovak or Czechoslovak-Polish tie would compensate the Soviets for the loss of peripheral (including Baltic) republics, all the more so were the just-outlined limit on sovereignty within the framework of a more than international-legal and less than confederal relationship to serve as a model for future ties with secession-prone republics to the Soviet Union. If Czechoslovakia and perhaps also Poland proved willing to limit a just achieved independence in relations with both Germany and Russia in so elastic a fashion that the more self-limiting the constitutional order of the former becomes, the looser the strategic ties to the latter could safely be, they might add domestic to environmental pressures on the Bonn Republic to adopt the corresponding constitutional revision as the one convincing token of readiness to extend effective assurance of safety to its eastern neighbors. Thus, to implement a species of "eastern Locarno" (one that failed to materialize between the wars) meant conceding the requisite guarantee in a manner complementing integration in the West, while adjusted to the still less trustworthy dispositions and conditions in the East.

Finally, in a historical-philosophical view, the proposed kind of reorganization would draw consequences from the regression of the wholly sovereign territorial-national state in today's Europe. It would do so in favor of updating the only alternative: a premodern model of vertically graduated authority. Both within and between time-given primary political formations (empires or states), spatially or organizationally delimited aggregations of interest would then be endowed with degrees of autonomy inversely related to the intensity of interactions among the units. The manifest cost is the complexity of structures and competencies, in the suggested contemporary context both intra- and international, as well as of the dually oriented links: to Germany and to Russia in East-Central Europe, just as to Russia and a Scandinavian complex in the north. However, because the organization merely expresses the existential complexity of both political problems and socio-political organisms, its complicated character is not only mandatory, but also beneficial.

It is both also insofar as it conforms to the transition from unilateral or reciprocal military-political security to multilaterally shared politico-economic stability as henceforth the focal concern of organization and primordial aim of strategy. Stability in East-Central Europe is underpinned when aggressively dynamic foreign activity by the more powerful states has been made impossible by a constitutional order that gives full rein to local divergences and disparate provincial priorities within both in the interest of widest possible self-determination.

VIII

A return to the medieval pattern could follow naturally from the decline of the state and the provisional end of the modern system international relations centered on the land-sea power conflict, of which the Cold War was the latest, if not necessarily the last. If such a transformation of global politics implies a need to institutionalize the renewed tendency toward graduated pluralism and locate its antecedents in time, it entails also the need to supplement the vertical pluralism with a horizontal dimension in space.

Beginning with Joachim of Flora and continuing through Vico to (with an insignificant addition) Marx, it has been the common property of philosophers of history to view the interplay of past with present as a prelude to the future in the form of three ages of the human drama. Following their example for the sake of disarticulating European history offers two possibilities. One is to view the ongoing economic West European renascence as culminating an evolution begun in the early-medieval cultural and spiritual Carolingian renaissance and continued (in the "second" age) through the triangular oceanic-continental struggles over politico-military and economic primacy, attending the modern era's symbiosis of territoriality with nationality. The (presently) culminating third age, wherein materialism has completed the triumph of secularism over religious spirituality, is then twice revolutionary. It signifies a reversal from the primacy of military into economic power, at the cost of forfeiting the manifold creativity of openly warlike contentions in favor of inherently sterile forms of lower-order violence, and it signals a like lowering for the attendant reversal that took place when the universal plane in cosmic hierarchy was transmuted from spiritual unity into unified world economy, while the contemporary analogue of the economic localism underpinning the earlier ecumene—the normative fragmentation brought on by religious and cultural fundamentalism—has made the modern functional equivalent of unity more fragile.

The other possibility is to leave to a continuing evolution the job of correcting present deficiencies in tomorrow's provisionally "third" age, one capable of reemplacing community values on top of the institutions that have issued from narrowly politico-economic revolutions. The age of feudalism has in such a view secreted into the present era of a socially aware welfare capitalism that successfully barred socialism's triumph by absorbing the latter's humanely progressive elements. Accordingly, extending the trajectory of historical materialism (in keeping with Hegel's open-ended idealistic scheme) adds history's to all other ironies insofar as the obverse of the predicted course of events supports the analytical structure of Marx's thought, even while Lenin's organizational practices go down in defeat. Were, however, international order to climax in the unequivocal triumph of nothing more significant than a somewhat retouched *laissez-faire*, materialism would be raised from co-creator of liberal institutions in the West to principal stimulus behind efforts to realize the ideal of political freedom in the impoverished parts of Europe as it were overnight. Succumbing to materialism while its theoretical formulation in collectivist totalitarian clothing is barely extinct would amount to an unredeemable betrayal of the West's innermost meaning. It came into and was being kept alive by the unique aptitude to convert into positive deeds the vital tension between what was and could be materially and what was not but had to be spiritually.

What does this signify? It means that the quality of a future "third" age is inseparable from the quality of a spirituality that deepens a merely economic renascence. At issue, then, is how and with what to elevate the moral tone of an inherently materialistic society to that of genuine community while it emerges out of the late humbling of the state, an institution that itself issued from the womb of a spirituality organized ecclesiatically to (and through the capacity to) correct economic scarcity sufficiently to curb religious excess; how and with what to replace the thwarted attempt of the totalitarian Right and Left ideologies to consummate history by absorbing, while pseudo-spiritually enhancing, previously dominant state types: one by resuscitating the sacral military monarchy of the Middle Ages; the other, by superseding the mercantile oligarchies of the modern era.

However, before we can begin to speculate what kind of spirituality is still within the reach of modern political man, we must ask where it could originate. It may not be only regional conceit—the psychologist's overcompensation—to identify the one remaining source in the parts of Europe once again (because not for the first time) impoverished to the profit of the Atlantic West after intercepting inroads from a still farther, Asiatic East—lately in the guise of the Stalinist variant of oriental despotism. The politically congealed and thus preserved creative energies and long unusable abilities of the East-Central and Eastern Europeans are their one possible contribution, as indispensable for the West as it was mandatory for the East if it is to accept the former's substantive assistance as one that honors a claim founded in the past and anticipates a right to be upheld by future accomplishment.

Is the possibility of such a spiritual contribution more than symbolically conveyed by the exceptionally important role

creative artists have played in the just-transpired East
European revolutions? Not quite, because statecraft as art even
more than science is an activity of a different and higher kind
than are the so-called creative arts. It must shape human
materials that are more fluid than is the painter's or the
sculptor's medium, within an ambience more difficult to
control than is the dramatist's freely prescribed dialogue for
the actor or the composer's notes for the musician. Alternately,
is such a spiritual contribution latent in the pan-European
idealism currently pervading both the public and the politics
in East-Central Europe? Again not sufficiently, insofar as the
mood is mechanical not only as the automatic reaction to immediate past, but also and more significantly in terms of both
time and space: temporally, when the illusionist would segre-
gate the present from the past by as radical a dividing line as
is the ensuing futurism; spatially, when the illusionist would
replace ideologically and militarily antithetical blocs with
parallel belts or zones of small countries interposed between
greater powers as the substitute basis of stability. This futurist
utopia denies future's issuance from a past to be continually
revalued to fit the needs of the present. Similar interpenetration
in space is ruled out by any effort to organize political geography in parallels that block a step-by-step growth of stability
into solidarity from narrower into larger circles with a common
center.

IX

Territorially parallel entities with political power entail confrontation as strength seeks to penetrate into the zone of
relative weakness from adjoining sides, just as the zone that
harbors a threatening power invites encirclement. The first
tendency portends the greater predicament for a belt of small
states between Germany and Russia should it materialize. Even
if economically coherent, such a coalition would, in terms of
power politics, constitute an inadequate arithmetical sum of its
constituent parts rather than an organic fusing of the parts into

a whole. It is, therefore, necessary to transform parallelism into concentrism of small with larger circles, first as a thought experiment. Concentricity makes it possible to evade confrontation in favor of consolidation when the recoiling from the greater power by smaller power—the motivational core of balancing dynamic—is countered by the power of attraction of the more effective economies, while the variable of extant cultural affinities can be such as to make the equation come out in favor of overall psychopolitical equilibrium.

Accordingly, if strategy is to constrain power differences and leaven material with cultural integration, and broaden community from narrower to wider circumferences in the process, it is not enough for tradition realism to amend fashionable utopias. In addition, cultural romanticism must vivify crabbed *Realpolitik* and humanize abstracted *Machtpolitik* if the compartmentalization of statesmanship into deformed constituents of its enlightened variety is to be undone. In East-Central Europe, this means putting the Slavs-respecting German, Herder, in Hitler's place, and, more generally, it means reforming interstate realtions by fusing properly construed Machiavellism with Mazzininian cultural syncretism, instead of projecting into relations among states the Leninist exacerbation of Marxism among classes. Only in some such fashion can politics return to the point from which it lost its way into mythologizing fascism and a "scientific" socialism spawned by rationalistic liberalism.

Reuniting reason with feeling means enabling fellow-feeling born of cultural affinities to substitute for tragic compassion, while easing the weight of power-political competition. And to make the substitution a responsibility for both major and minor states in their foreign politics means more than lifting the prosaic transactions of routine diplomacy to the humane concerns of reformist ecology. A higher but still political plane can be ascended when the organizational forms of the "first" (universalist-feudal) age of diversity have been allowed to temper the excesses of the "second" (territorial-statist) age of centralization. This will require complementing the vertically graduated pluralism of intra- and interstate organisms that represent different interests through complementarily ordered jurisdictional competencies, with a horizontally configured plurality of politically, economically, and culturally inter-penetrating regional and supraregional circles or spheres.

In an East-Central Europe marked by uneven potencies and potential, preparing for a "third" age may therefore mean filling constitutional forms modeled on medieval and still earlier institutions with cultural modes of thought and emotion originating in late the eighteenth and nineteenth centuries. This does not necessarily mean replicating the abortive efforts at satisfying the Slavs within a reconstructed monarchy during an earlier postrevolutionary era, after 1848. For one thing, the ongoing evolution inside the Soviet successor to tsarist des-potism has meanwhile weakened formerly valid objections to turning instead to Russophile pan-Slavism. For another, the danger from a species of Germanism that activates not so much political and military as economic and cultural imperialism has not been comparably extinguished. Both changes call for an adaptation of the earlier model.

Within a roughly concentric pattern of regional, continental, and global spheres, Czechoslovakia forms with Poland the center of the smallest circle bounded by Germany and Russia; Germany is at the center of the next larger one, comprising Europe west and east; and classic Europe is poised to become again the focus of the largest sphere, encompassing the eastern and western hemispheres. Implicit in the pattern are the prime foreign policy tasks for the two west-Slavic countries of the northern tier. To fit the configuration, the policies have to be directed to independence-within-interdependence with respect to Russia and Germany on the regional plane, to equality of the eastern with the western region of Europe on the continen-tal plane, and to overall stability on the Eurocentric global plane. The diplomatic objectives are complementary and the implementing strategies feasible to the extent that the three spheres are themselves functionally linked. Thus, active in-volvement in the regional inner sphere by the United States and Japan from the outer global sphere is both sufficient and necessary to compensate for Russia's economic weakness, diversify Germany's economic attractiveness, and solidify Russia's strategic position between Germany and China. And an only parallel or also coordinated involvement of the two outsiders in consolidating the regional sphere into a community concurrently helps restrain the growth of U.S.-Japanese economic rivalry from emerging disruptively now that it is no longer suppressed by U.S.-Soviet competition. The same applies to the advantages of France's and England's involvement, from the intermediate all-European sphere on the eastern side of the two-way street to the inhibitions against the revival of interwar Anglo-French strategic divergencies or threats to postwar Franco-German community building on its western side.

Because Czechoslovakia and Poland find themselves at or near both the physical and functional center of a concentrically articulated horizontal geographic pluralism, which brings down to earth from the heavens the pluri-spheric medieval cosmography, this enhances the potential and reduces the risks of their role in graduated vertical pluralism that updates past relationships to the "holy" empire. The position implies marked improvement on the historic condition of both countries, and of the Czech lands in particular, which were heretofore the only passive objects or also victims in a space organized in function of parallel politico-economic zones and representative types of powers spread along the ever-widening west-to-east insular-amphibious-rear continental spectrum, which has culminated in the American-Soviet-Chinese triangle. Were that pattern to be reconstituted in the reverse, east-to-west, direction, with a Japanese-American-Russian or Chinese–classic European triangle, East-Central Europe would be placed no more favorably than if the Cold War pattern were to be reactivated. The area would return to being the dependent adjunct of the dominant Eurasian would-be amphibian, or regress into the most forward and thus no less vulnerable extension of a classic Europe that was pushed back into the onerous rear-continental posture without necessarily being able to implement the posture's strategically crucial role. In either posture, it would be beyond the reach of the extra-European powers.

Yet organizing now "Central" Europe on the basis of a north-to-south belt or zone of small states parallel with adjoining aggregations of greater (or differently fragmented) power would mean fostering this unpromising prospect. Such an arrangement would do more than inhibit the evolution of the region's northern tier toward community via an institutionalized dynamic equilibrium, which is open in the concentric structural alternative. It would also brake positive developments inside the intermediate continental and the outer global spheres insofar as the tendency toward either power vacuum or local great-power condominium, latent in parallelism, diminishes the region's potential to attract outside parties into involvement, offer them open access, and exercise leverage on them to engage locally.

If the foreign policy of a small state is to draw consequences from continuing dangers and novel opportunities, strategy must do justice to an equation that comprises sheer might, which repels (and necessitates a link to countervailing power), and economic potency, which attracts (and, requiring diversification in kind, can be politically neutralized only by means of cultural affinity). Applying the strategic equation for stability in relations with Germany and Russia does not require instantly identifying and precisely factoring its elements in terms of the threatening overweight and requisite counterweight, uneven attraction and mutual dependence in economics, different forms and expressions of cultural affinities, and temperamental propinquities vis-à-vis one or the other big neighbor. It is enough to have confidence in the strategy being feasible in concept and able in practice to generate a stability that can raise the spiritual level of member societies within a shared regional community, which, together with the one in the West, revitalized Europe as again the heart of a viable global organism.

CONCLUSION

VII

Old Thinking and New Realities: The Legacy of Postwar Realism

Michael T. Clark

T HE REVOLUTIONS OF 1989 brought down first walls, then long-standing policies and governments, and finally the assumptions upon which all these rested. In the process, nations that were enthralled have been liberated, one that was divided, made whole, and more: As the East-West conflict that has dominated international politics since the end of the World War II has dissipated, so too has the international order to which it gave rise.

For all these reasons, the end of the Cold War has rightly been hailed as an event of exceptional historical significance. Yet the long-term significance of the revolutions of 1989 and all that they spawned remains largely obscure. In part, this uncertainty is the consequence of the sheer pace, complexity, and pervasiveness of the transformations that have taken place in each of these separate dimensions. The drama of the past year has few historical parallels. In part, too, this indeterminacy is a reflection of the fact that the nature of whatever new international order is to be constructed from the ruins of the old will depend on the varied responses of a large number of independent and interdependent actors, each confronting new or unforeseen dilemmas in rapidly evolving circumstances. But the obscurity of present trends also reflects a more fundamental uncertainty: Is the process of change now sweeping the world merely a hopeful prelude to what in the end could appear as yet another succession crisis in the long history of the rise and decline of states? Or is this process of change nothing less than the transformation of the very pattern of international politics? Underlying and amplifying all of these uncertainties is the very large question of the future commitment of the United States to preserving the broader conditions that have brought this possibility of "real change" into being.

Have we indeed arrived at a turning point in the history of international society? As the other contributions to this volume make clear, the evidence for such a conclusion is mixed, but strong. The events of 1989 need not have signaled the arrival of the millenium to take on a large significance; all that was required is what, in fact, they have allowed—a glimpse beyond international politics as we have always known it to an era of modest enlightenment in which the possibility of radical and constructive change may coexist peacefully with the claims of state interest. What makes the present circumstance truly remarkable is the possibility that it portends, or at least makes thinkable, not only the end of an order that we have found increasingly burdensome and unsatisfying, but also (the beginning of) the end of history or at least of the kind of story the world has known until now: a chronicle dominated by conflict and competition, not cooperation, among the world's leading industrial states and punctuated with disturbing regularity by the outbreak of ever-more destructive war.

Because this prospect arises at a moment when the costs of America's postwar global role have become exceedingly difficult to bear and the rewards increasingly difficult to credit, it is not surprising that many citizens should look upon the possibility of a radical change in the nature and conditions of international society as if it were an accomplished fact. Policymakers may be justified in greeting such claims of novelty with wary skepticism. Yet the sheer magnitude of recent events has taken away the most powerful prima facie evidence for doubting the possibility of real change—the weight of experience—and has deprived our postwar policy of its principal rationale, which is the need to protect the international system from the predations of an expansionist Communist superpower. More important, the end of the Cold War has transformed our relations with our allies no less than with our former adversary and made it more difficult to exercise global leadership even as the rewards of such leadership have diminished.

Finally, the expectation that the end of the Cold War must bring with it the dawn of a new era in international politics is not one born of the hopes engendered by present circumstances. Rather, that promise has been held out since the foundations of postwar U.S. foreign policy were first articulated and set in place; it has provided a lodestar through more than four decades of Cold War and has served to justify the commitments undertaken and the sacrifices made by two generations of Americans. Its disappointment must have far-reaching consequences, not the least of which may be a refusal on the part of large sectors of the public to support similar calls for sacrifice and commitment in the future.

To recall the process by which the conditions for international change today were laid down, thus, is no mere academic exercise and still less an indulgence of self-congratulation, however justified such a pose may be. It is rather a duty imposed upon statesman and citizen alike by the momentous occurrences of the past year. And it is an indispensable task for determining what role the United States can and should play, and should understand itself to be playing, in a reconstructed international order.

II

It is not the fact, but the character, of contemporary change that demands attention. The measure of change must be comparative; to evaluate the significance of the present pattern of change, it is necessary to consider the traditional pattern.

Change in international society has been as unavoidable as it has been irregular. Traditionally, it has taken place in only two distinct dimensions, yet has always been at least possible in two others. The first dimension is delimited by the spatial or geographic distribution of power and, with power, such authority as exists in international society. The second dimension is defined by the interests and norms that govern interactions and serve to moderate or exacerbate conflict. Change in the first dimension is measured by asking, "Which political entities now

exercise the greatest influence?" In the second, change is measured by posing the question, "what new demands are placed
on the conduct of statecraft?" not, "who wields authority?" but
"under what conditions and constraints?"

That the revolutions already begun in Eastern Europe and
those under way in the Soviet Union, in Germany, and in the
consolidating European Community portend far-reaching
change in both these dimensions of international order is by
now obvious, even though the ultimate consequences of these
events remain highly uncertain. The rise and decline of states
(including the United States), their amalgamation (as seems
certain in Western Europe), or disintegration (as may be
occurring in the Soviet Union) has long been the stuff of
international politics. And the general implications, if not the
specific results, of such systemic transformations are both
understandable and predictable because they have all been
seen before. Thus, although it cannot yet be told whether the
events of the past year spell the end of the Soviet Union as a
great state, it is already evident that the end of the Cold War
has altered the position of both superpowers in the world and
that the dissolution of the Communist bloc in Eastern Europe
has redefined the circumstances in which the states of all parts
of Europe interact.

There is a sense, however, that the changes in the distribution of power or the specific terms of international intercourse
now taking place have had little impact on the underlying
conditions of interstate politics. During the history of the
modern state system, dated by scholarly tradition from the
Treaty of Westphalia (1648), which ended Reformation
Europe's protracted religious wars and implicitly recognized
the institution of the state as supreme sovereign in its territory,
no reassignment of roles and no modification of the rules of
international conduct has altered the most fundamental condition of international life—the absence of a lawful authority
above the national sovereigns—or its baleful consequences: the
radical insecurity of states, and the prevalence of self-help, and,
hence, the resort to force as the chief means of attaining

security and arbitrating conflict within the international system. In short, although particular orders—defined by the specific assignment of roles and rules among always hierarchically ranked states—have come and gone, the system of international politics has remained in essential respects the same. The possibility of modifying this aboriginal condition of international life and thereby attenuating its evils represents a third, but at least until now only potential, dimension of change.

A fourth possible dimension of change is represented by the way men and women think about international society and politics. The hope, and for many the promise, of the new age ushered in by the revolutions of 1989 and following is that they may make it possible not only to conceive, but also to act upon, "new thinking" in international affairs. Here, of course, an important distinction must be made between what people say and what they do. If the essence of "new thinking" is defined by the search for an alternative to that most traditional method of enhancing the security and prosperity of the nation—that is, war or the threat of it—then neither the impetus toward nor the claim of "new thinking" are truly novel. Moreover, if what is said is an accurate guide to what is thought, then there have been very few Machiavellians in history. But if what policy-makers do is a clearer guide to what they really think, then a great many statesmen, and nearly all effective ones, have been Machiavellians. Taking the behavior of statesmen—what they have been willing to countenance and unwilling to eschew in the interests of their states—and taking the actions of the mediocre mass rather than the exemplary few as the most reliable indicators of historical continuity, it is evident that change in this dimension, too, so far has been only potential.

Yet it is precisely because the changes of the past year have been heralded as auguring a change in these last dimensions of international politics that it has become necessary to ask whether something more profound is afoot. The present process of change is distinguished from previous patterns by its pace and comprehensiveness—and even more by its general peacefulness.

In the past, transformations of international order on the scale of the one now unfolding have been the result of great conflicts and great wars. The present change, too, follows a great conflict and war, but a conflict that, however earnestly it was contested, remained muted and a war that, however frightening it sometimes became, remained "cold."

The general question these facts raise is whether they represent merely an unusual resolution of a traditional pattern of international relations—or reflect, as advocates of "new thinking" insist, an acceptance of and accommodation to more fundamental change in the pattern of international politics. For U.S. citizens, the more immediate question change poses is whether the new circumstances created by the waning of the postwar Soviet-American conflict permit an escape from the burdens of international involvement imposed by the Cold War on U.S. statecraft. To assess the significance of contemporary change and gauge what is to come or may yet be brought into being at these deeper levels of possibility, however, it is necessary to consider first what has been. And to test the claims of "new thinking," it is necessary first to recall the rationale of "old thinking."

III

What is "old thinking"? What commitments and assumptions define the traditional outlook and approach that the "new thinkers" claim to reject? If the claims of novelty are to be understood and evaluated, the rationale of the *ancien système* of global politics must be given its due.

Heretofore the distinguishing characteristic of all successful statecraft has been its realism. This statement is almost a tautology. It would be a tautology if realism were understood to mean nothing more than a pragmatic adjustment to circumstance and if success meant nothing more than the protection of a state's vital interests—above all, its interests in its own security and survival. Understood this way, the statement would be neither a syllogism nor an axiom, but a barely disguised (and barely meaningful) identity of terms. As a doctrine informing the practice of statecraft, however, realism has meant something more specific—a distinctive view of the necessary methods and of the generally practicable ends of statecraft—and success has been defined as something more than the preservation of the physical integrity of the nation. Because realism does imply a specific kind of response—in thought, as well as practice—to the enduring conditions of national life, the statement that realism, or "old thinking," has been a condition of political success provides telling evidence of the necessities historically imposed on statecraft by the nature of international society.

In its classical expressions in the writings of traditional philosophers of international politics as diverse as the ancient Athenian historian Thucydides, the Renaissance Florentine epigramist Niccolò Machiavelli, the seventeenth-century English philosopher Thomas Hobbes and the early twentieth-century German political sociologist Max Weber, realism, or "old thinking," has been consistently marked by three essential features. The first and most basic is a commitment to the preservation of the state at virtually any cost.[1] Realists are distinguished by the high, virtually supreme, value they assign to the security, independence, and survival of the state. In weighing values, and faced with a choice between violating some basic norm of human conduct and sacrificing a vital interest of the state, they invariably opt for the former to avoid the latter. Indeed, in Machiavelli's notorious formulation of this principle, there seems to be nothing that cannot be done or justified in the name of the state: "For when the safety of one's country wholly depends on the decision to be taken, no attention should be paid to justice or injustice, to kindness or cruelty, or to its being praiseworthy or ignominious. On the contrary, every other consideration being set aside, that alternative should be wholeheartedly adopted

---

1. My understanding of political realism owes much to the teaching and writings of George Liska and Robert W. Tucker.

which will save the life and preserve the freedom of one's country."[2]

Remarks such as this have often led scholars to conclude that for realists the preservation of the state represents not merely a high value, but *the* highest value. Unless qualified, however, the conclusion is unwarranted. The notion that the vital interests of the state carry great weight, even moral weight, has often proved compatible with the idea that the state as an institution has no inherent moral worth. Thus, even so ardent a nationalist as Weber could insist "it is possible to defend quite meaningfully the view that the power of the state should be increased in order to strengthen its power to overcome obstacles, while maintaining that the state itself has no *intrinsic* value, that it is a purely technical instrument for the realization of other values from which alone it derives its value, and that it can retain this value only as long as it does not seek to transcend this merely auxiliary status."[3]

---

2. *The Discourses*, Book III, Chapter 41 (Baltimore: Penguin Books, 1970), 515. Machiavelli does not say, it should be observed, that anything that serves the interest of the state is justified. Even in the passage quoted here, perhaps among the most frequently cited in his entire corpus, he insists only that ordinary moral considerations can be set aside when the life and freedom of the state are at issue. All but the most absolute moralists would seem to concede this point in principle, which seems to restrict the problem of reason of state within the narrow bounds of extreme emergency. The real difficulty arises, however, when it comes to specifying which actions cannot be done in such circumstances and in defining just what it is that defines the life and freedom of the political community. If Machiavelli's doctrine is to be distinguished from conventional moral wisdom, it is not simply because of his willingness to sacrifice moral values for the survival of the state and the values that it serves to protect, but because of his frank refusal to set any limits to what might be done in such circumstances—provided they are necessary—and because of the wide latitude he gave to defining what is "necessary" to secure the state's vitality and independence.

3. "The Meaning of 'Ethical Neutrality'" in Max Weber, *The Methodology of the Social Sciences*, Edward A. Shils and Henry A. Finch, trans. (New York: The Free Press, 1949), 47.

A rejection of the idea of the moral dignity of the state, hence, is not at all tantamount to a rejection of the idea that its requirements may override virtually every other moral consideration. For even where the moral value of the state is understood to be purely derivative, a means to an end, as long as the end that the state serves is itself a high value and as long as the state is the indispensable means of securing that value, the value assigned to the preservation of the state may be practically indistinguishable from the value the state serves to protect and enhance.

The second distinctive feature of traditional thought, or realism, is a premise of the first: namely, a conviction that the security and independence of the state are indispensable for realizing the fundamental values of the political community. The point is not that all values are realized or enhanced through the medium of the state, nor even that any of them derive from the state, but that in the absence of a secure state, no other value can be secure. So long as the political organization of the world is dominated by sovereign entities without an effective supra-national organ to guarantee their survival and independence for them, national communities are forced to rely upon the organized force of their own political institutions for such protection and aid as they can be made to provide.

The reason that the preservation of the state forms the primary end of statecraft is that in a world of sovereign states, the fundamental rights, including the right to exist, of a national community must remain uncertain. In a world in which there is no other guarantee of the preservation of a community apart from the collective force of the community itself, the protective institutions of the state have provided the most dependable and, too often, the only meaningful measure of security.

If the vital functions that the state performs could be served more effectively by other means, of course, the moral value assigned to the state could scarcely be maintained. But in the absence of a more reliable means of fulfilling this essential function of providing security for the community, the state has been and must remain indispensable for preserving the essential conditions of national life. It is for want of an effective alternative to the ordering and protective institutions of the state that the interests of those institutions has often assumed the weight of moral necessity. And it is this quasi-moral character of the state's necessity that has always given urgency to the claim of reason of state.

The third characteristic feature of realism is betrayed in its distinctive approach to international order. Statesmen of all perspectives, of course, have seldom been content to restrict their view of success in statecraft to the simple preservation of the physical integrity of the institutions and territory of the national state. In part, this is because the security interests that the state has served to protect have never been limited to the physical integrity of the community alone. Great states especially, but all states generally—and some to a degree not always commensurate with their power—have been reluctant to define as threats to national independence and survival only those acts that immediately and directly impinge upon the citizens or territory of the nation.[4] In part, also, political leaders have taken an expansive view of their security interests because the values that a state aims to protect are seldom understood to be those of the national community alone.[5] Most broadly, statesmen have

---

4. That even small states may take an expansive view of security was demonstrated during the October 1983 crisis in the Caribbean nation of Grenada. After the violent coup in which Prime Minister Maurice Bishop was overthrown and then executed by members of his own New Jewel Movement government, the neighboring states of the Organization of Eastern Caribbean States (OECS) perceived an imminent threat to their own safety in the "climate of uncertainty" created by the violence. The fact that the resulting government was isolated even at home and lacked both a motive and a capacity to export its upheaval across the sea did not deter the OECS countries from declaring a threat to their collective security or prevent the United States from acting on that claim.

5. In the classic case of America's entry into World War II, for example, it was difficult to make the case that Hitler's aggression in Europe threatened the physical integrity of the United States or directly impinged upon the institutions of U.S. society. Yet, the fear of being isolated in world dominated by fascist power was more than enough to encourage the Roosevelt ad-

seldom been content to restrict their consideration of policy to the circumstances of the moment, but have sought both to reduce the immediacy of standing threats and to anticipate and avert the emergence of new ones. To this end, they invariably have been drawn to shape the larger environment in which the state must survive and prosper and to strengthen the foundations of a more general order in which their own security is enhanced by the interest that others share in preserving that order.

Specific "milieu goals" have varied with the particular moral preferences and political capacities of different societies, of course. And the value-content of these goals have often carried grave moral significance, as well as large political implications. Yet, the pursuit of international order per se hardly distinguishes "new" thinking from "old," and the desire to create a "congenial environment" for the realization of a nation's values has been a desideratum of nearly all statecraft, traditional or otherwise.

What has distinguished realistic statecraft from other varieties has been its specific understanding of the necessary conditions of international order and, hence, its distinctive criteria of success. The traditional approach to international order has proceeded from a recognition that the order that a world of states has proven capable of achieving is a kind of divisive order. Because lines are drawn to define and delimit the national community protected by a state, they also serve to separate that community from all others; the Westphalian territorial compromise—*cuius regio, eius religio*—bought peace at the expense of the idea of a shared community of value. Thus, the solidarity achieved, however deep, within the boundaries of the state is thus necessarily limited in geographic scope. And, in consequence, the

---

ministration to do all it thought it could to prevent Britain's defeat and led many citizens to demand that it do more. Hitler's declaration of war on the United States after the Japanese attack on Pearl Harbor settled the issue as far as public opinion was concerned. Yet historians today still find it difficult to demonstrate how a Nazi victory in Europe would have impaired the physical security of the United States.

values and interests that any international order could be expected to serve were limited to those that were common to all—or at least to all those whose participation counts.

At the same time, such security as international society has achieved has been purchased at an extreme price. The ultimate price of security has always been war, and success in war has regularly proven to be the only sure guarantee of rights. Order in international society, in short, has been guaranteed ultimately by the willingness of states to go to war or threaten war. The fact that the order achieved among independent sovereigns has been subject to frequent and severe disruption has inclined those responsible for the security of their states to maintain a posture of constant readiness. If the nature of war, as Hobbes once observed, "consisteth not in actual fighting; but in the known disposition thereto; during all the time there is no assurance to the contrary,"[6] then it is difficult to contradict the assertion that the states system has been in practice a war system. In such a system, realists have concluded, political order is necessarily an order defined by power.

This conclusion, moreover, has undermined the expectation that international order can be made to reflect any profound conception of justice. "Right, as the world goes," Thucydides records the Athenians saying at Melos, "is in question only between equals in power, while the strong do what they can and the weak suffer what they must."[7] This statement, which sounds so cynical on first hearing, has often been interpreted as an attempt to place moral considerations beyond the purview of diplomacy. But in view of the conditions that have traditionally governed international life, it may read better as a factual statement about the political and moral realities of a world of states. Although frequently condemned by critics of Athenian policy as a rejection of all moral principle in the

---

6. *Leviathan*, Chapter 13 (Oxford: Basil Blackwell, n.d. [1957]), 82.

7. *The Peloponnesian War*, Book V, Chapter 89, Edward Crawley, trans. (New York: Modern Library, 1982), 351.

relations of states, the observation attributed to the Athenian representatives was surely intended by its authors as a warning to those who would seek justice without first attending to the facts of power. By the same token, however, the punishment meted out to the Melians by the Athenians for their failure to accommodate to a supposed law of nature—the execution of every male citizen of military age—reveals what even the flower of Western civilization has done, and felt justified doing, when confronted with a threat to its vital state interests.

IV

It is not least among the ironies of our present situation that what has contributed most to the revolutions of 1989 and, thus, to the prospect of an emerging era of "new thinking" in international society has been a determined application of the quintessential principles of the traditional practice of statecraft. For better or worse, and more often implicitly than explicitly, the strategy that has seen the United States and its allies through the Cold War has been one that conforms in all essential aspects with the recommendations of classical realism. In the case of the United States especially, this has required more than an adaptation of principles to special circumstances. It has implied the subordination in practice, and the accommodation in thought, of a unique view of national purpose— our self-defined and self-defining mission to bring the benefits of individual rights and economic liberty to a benighted world—to the more prosaic tasks of constructing and preserving an international balance of power.

That such an accommodation should have proven especially difficult, often discomfiting, and ultimately incomplete in the U.S. case is not surprising. What is surprising is that it could be done at all, so alien to the American way of thinking about the world are the assumptions and expectations that have traditionally guided statecraft. One might have expected that the distinctive nature of the values that the American state has always been understood to protect and that presumably guide our conduct would have set limits to the means and imposed constraints on the kinds of actions to which our national leaders would have recourse. After all, the fundamental purpose of American society—our commitment to the protection and enhancement of equality of rights and to the extension of economic freedom—were and are virtually defined in opposition to the claims of state interest.

In its moral core, the American reason of state has always been anti–reason of state. Moreover, the nation's unique experience of security, which in turn reflected the uniquely benign circumstances in which the country expanded and prospered, has added the weight of experience to the ideological conviction in the American mind that the traditional claims of state interest reflect an atavism, the elimination of whose every remnant expression must be among our most enduring concerns. Finally, this conception of our role in history has been so intimately connected to our sense of who and what we are, it has proven almost inevitable that when we have elected to play an active part in world affairs, we have felt compelled to reconcile our actions with this special mission.

These considerations might have been expected to impede our accommodation to the traditional practices and standards of statecraft or at least make our adjustment to the requirements of circumstance a painful and arduous process. Looking back, however, on what was done, rather than what was aimed for (or was said to be the aim), and on what means were employed and with what expectations, it is hard to demonstrate that our principled opposition to the ancient claims of reason of state served to inhibit our behavior in any profound way.

Certainly with respect to the claims of state interest, the postwar era has witnessed an expansion of the authority of government far beyond anything contemplated, much less

witnessed, in our previous history.[8] The expansion and reorganization of the executive and its ascendancy over Congress;
the creation of large, powerful, and secret agencies as part of
a new national security apparatus; the maintenance of a
standing army (or "forces-in-being") numbering millions; and
the emergence of what President Dwight Eisenhower described
in his farewell address as an unprecedented "conjunction of an
immense military establishment and a large arms industry"
integrated in a vast "military-industrial complex"—all these
developments point to the acceptance in practice, if not in
principle, of the primacy of the state and of its interests. Max
Weber would have recognized the national security state for
what it was: a *Machtstaat*, or power state, aimed at unifying
and enlarging the resources of the society for the purposes of
advancing the national interest.

The degree to which the domestic institutions of U.S.
society were transformed—all in the space of less than a
decade after World War II—provides powerful testimony of
the ease with which even the most embedded ideological
convictions can be swept aside by circumstance. But there is
other evidence as well. No principle of foreign policy seems to
have been more rooted in the traditional U.S. conception of

---

8. It may be observed against the view presented here that the acceptance of large claims of state interest proceeded hand in hand with the
development of big government as a response to the Great Depression and
that, therefore, the expansion of the claims of state interest has other roots
besides the need to adjust to the requirements of America's new international
role. Certainly it must be true that the expansion of the role of the state in
national life was made easier by the precedent of the New Deal. Yet although
the emergence of the national security state and of the welfare state may be
linked in time, they have always answered to separate rationales, and the
acceptance of one has not necessarily required the acceptance of the other. As
the events of the 1980s made palpably clear and the present budget impasse
confirms, rejection of big government in the form of the welfare state is
hardly tantamount to the rejection of big government in the form of the
national security state; conversely, rejection of the larger claims of state
interest advanced in the name of national security has never been understood
to require a denial of the claims of state interest on behalf of social welfare.

limited state authority or more confirmed by experience than that first given expression in George Washington's farewell address and later summarized by Thomas Jefferson as "peace, commerce, and honest friendship, with all nations—entangling alliances with none."

In part, this principle was motivated by a realistic and nationalistic recognition that to embroil the country in the quarrels of powerful states far across the sea would be a policy justified neither by interest nor by political necessity. In part, however, it was recognized that to fulfill the obligations of alliance or at least minimize its risks, precisely the kinds of institutional changes that were initiated after World War II would be required, and these, in turn, it was feared (not entirely without justification, as we now know) would have corrosive effects on the American political system, including the subversion of the balance between the executive and legislative branches; a reduction of official accountability; the abuse of public authority; the growth of national debt; and, as a consequence of all these, a weakening of both industry and civic commitment. By convention, the decision to accept the Atlantic Alliance and all that it implied is held to be one of the "great debates" of twentieth-century U.S. history. Considering all the consequences of the decision that was made, however, what is most striking about the argument about our commitment to the military defense of Western Europe is how quickly—and finally—it was settled and how little close scrutiny was given to the notion that our own national security made such an involvement necessary.

If the transformation of U.S. federal institutions and our adoption of the one act of foreign policy that seemed debarred by both conviction and experience show how far the claims of state interest were allowed to expand in the early postwar era, nothing so clearly illustrates our acceptance of the claims of reason of state in practice as the doctrine and programs of nuclear deterrence. In its essence, the doctrine of nuclear deterrence, like the pure plea of reason of state, draws an equation between the evil that is threatened and the value that must be protected. What makes deterrence a particularly acute expression of the ancient plea is the extremity of the evil that must be weighed against the interests to be protected. Given the evil that can be expected to result from a nuclear war, even if the destruction of such a war could be limited to those who are unambiguously the aggressors (an assumption that was always doubtful and has become only more doubtful in the past 40 years), deterrence stretches this equation to lengths that people could not even have imagined in the centuries before our own. Moreover, given the high probability that in the event of a nuclear war the values destroyed would include many of those for which deterrence was deemed justified, modern deterrence carries the ancient plea of state necessity to moral lengths never before contemplated and may even constitute its *reductio ad absurdum.*

It may be, and frequently has been, denied that the U.S. adoption of a deterrent strategy expresses the ancient plea that where the survival and security of the state are at risk, no means, however ignominious or cruel, should be avoided that may preserve the life or freedom of the state. It has been denied on the grounds that a threat to use extreme means is not quite the same thing as the actual use of those means. It has been denied because the aim of deterrence is said to be preventive, not aggressive. And it has been denied that deterrence conforms to the plea of necessity of state because it is justified not on the grounds of state or national interest, or at least not on these grounds alone, but by the larger interest of preserving international order upon the which the fate of all states and thus, nearly all other values depends.

All of these denials fail to convince, however, because they fail to consider the moral calculus that has been and is required to make deterrence work. In the first instance, it is true that deterrence is a threat to commit a great evil and is not the evil itself. But it is equally true that the threat would carry no force if it did not also carry conviction that the implicit moral calculation is valid, and, what is more, where that conviction is present, the possibility that one may indeed act upon it cannot be ruled out. Indeed, a threat that is only a threat and does not reflect a conviction that the threatened action would be justified, can hardly serve to deter.[9] In the second instance, the moral quality of the act contemplated or threatened surely depends upon more than the purpose the act is intended to serve; the justification of deterrence must also rest upon the judgment that the destruction expected to result from the use of nuclear weapons is outweighed by the nature of the evil to be repelled. Again, deterrence can only be effective, and so preventive, where the will is strengthened by the conviction that the use of nuclear arms would be justified to repel aggression.

Finally, if the threat of nuclear war is justified by principles greater than the national interest, it must mean that the international order it serves to defend is justified by something more than state interest—that is, that it carries in its

---

9. This problem undermines all so-called existential doctrines of deterrence—theories that hold that the mere existence of nuclear weapons creates an uncertainty whose dangers are so grave that nations confronting a nuclear-armed state will be reluctant to employ their military power against it, even where it seems unlikely that the nuclear weapons would be employed. The attractiveness of these doctrines is both material and moral: They seem to allow a "minimal" deployment of weapons, one less dependent upon the action of the other side and so less conducive to arms races (and so, it also appears, less provocative) and to circumvent the moral equation of more conventional theories of deterrence. But uncertainty has minimal as well as maximal requirements: Proponents of existential theories emphasize the maximum requirements, while ignoring its minimum conditions. Where agreement with the other side is not possible (that is, in the circumstances of the Cold War), however, to maintain a condition of uncertainty requires at least some minimal proportion of balance. Because a deterrent whose use could only result in vast destruction, including the destruction of one's homeland, would be neither moral nor effective, even a minimal posture can be quite large and would need to be responsive to the actions of the other side. On the moral side, where there is conviction that use of nuclear weapons is wrong, it is to be wondered how deployment alone can serve to deter, or is even justified, given the risks of preemptive or preventive attack that must attend any level deployment.

institutions some other, broader principles of justice. Otherwise, what would it mean to insist that the international order represents a moral value sufficient to justify a resort to nuclear arms in its defense?

This last question begs another: In what way has the postwar order been an order of justice? Certainly not in its inception. Merely to mention the names of Yalta and Potsdam and the great power agreements reached in those cities is to recall the illegitimate origins of the postwar dispensation. If, apart from its origins, the postwar order eventually came to reflect a principle of legitimacy, and so to approximate justice, we have never acknowledged this. To the contrary, we steadfastly maintained throughout the Cold War that the Soviet position in Eastern Europe was illegitimate, and an important, perhaps the most important, obstacle to progress toward the establishment of a just international order. The mere implication, vigorously denied by its exponents, that the policy of détente implied an "immoral" acceptance of the postwar territorial settlement was sufficient to win that policy a wide array of opponents from all points on the U.S. political spectrum. Moreover, it has been often, and in the 1980s vehemently, denied that the postwar order constituted an order at all, for the very reason that it was founded on no principle higher than those of expediency and prudence.

The question, of course, is whether by our actions and policy we gave nevertheless gave tacit recognition to the postwar order. The existence of an order in international society has never been understood to depend upon moral approval, but upon acceptance of its rules and constraints. Was the postwar order an order in this sense? Here again, a distinction must be made between the aspirations that informed our policy and that facts that determined it, between what Paul Nitze once described as declaratory policy and action policy.

Reviewing our actions since 1945, it is difficult to resist the conclusion that, our many words to the contrary notwithstanding, in our actions, we did accept important constraints on our behavior and were willing for the sake of expediency to accommodate circumstances. This was the case not only in the era of détente: Our acceptance of constraints on policy in Eastern Europe both predated and survived détente's consolidation. After proclaiming "liberation" and "rollback" as the aims of U.S. policy in Eastern Europe and encouraging the Hungarian revolt of 1956, the Eisenhower administration stood by as Soviet tanks ruthlessly put down the first real challenge to the legitimacy of the postwar order.

Again in 1968, the Johnson administration, broken by its commitment to opposing "aggression" in Southeast Asia, did little more than watch and condemn as Czechoslovakia's Prague Spring was brutally crushed in August of 1968. Even as late as the mid-1980s, proponents of a more aggressive policy to combat Soviet expansionism in the cause of human freedom could insist that the Reagan Doctrine was "not the reckless— and toothless—call for reclaiming the core Soviet possessions in Eastern Europe, which the Soviets claim for self-defense and, more important, which they are prepared to use the most extreme means to retain."[10] To this extent, the postwar division of Europe had come to be accepted as an immutable, if illegitimate, fact.

The postwar order certainly lacked a common agreement on norms, yet it had its rules. And, if it failed by the criteria of domestic society, it nonetheless served well by the standards of international society. To the extent it was an order of deterrence, it was quintessentially an order of power; to the extent that it denied to the lesser powers the very basic right to national sovereignty and independence, it failed as an order of justice. Yet, it cannot for these reasons alone be denied that the postwar order was an order nonetheless, unless one is to apply to the problem of international order standards that the world has only rarely been able to observe. Just as the tolerance for disorder in international society has always been higher than in national society, so too the standards of order in inter-

---

10. Charles Krauthammer, "The Reagan Doctrine," *Time*, April 15, 1985.

national society have necessarily always been looser and more primitive than those of domestic society. If the principles to which the postwar order attained ran no higher than the dictates of prudence and expediency, these are precisely the "principles" that have always provided the most effective safeguards of order in international society. And it was our behavior, not our pronouncements that confirmed our acceptance of the postwar dispensation.

V

Together, these considerations illustrate the extent to which American policy in the post–World War II era conformed to the dictates and patterns of traditional, realistic statecraft. Do they also demonstrate the abandonment, or betrayal, in foreign policy of the American purpose? If not, how has it been possible to reconcile our behavior with the traditional conception of our global historic role? Has our real or pretended adherence to an idealistic mission provided just another illustration of the virtually unlimited pliability of ideology under the pressure of state interest? Or are there other ways to connect the policies we adopted and the ends we pursued? Most broadly, what are the grounds for supposing that a successful application of the traditional methods of statecraft may have served to open the door to a new era in international politics, an age characterized by ever-broader acceptance of "new thinking" in international politics?

In justifying the role that the United States played in upholding international order during the Cold War, it will not do to point out that this role was largely dictated by circumstances— that is, by the collapse of the indigenous European balance of power that had long been the condition of our security, the emergence of a totalitarian threat to international order in the form of our erstwhile Soviet ally, and the need to prevent the concentration of a preponderant share of the world's industrial potential in hostile hands. It will not do to argue this way because the role we played went far beyond what was required for our physical protection. More important, it will not do because we ourselves never justified our policy on the grounds of national security alone, but on the conviction that, as President Harry Truman put it in his appeal for aid to Greece and Turkey, ". . . it must be the policy of the United States to support free peoples who are resisting attempted subjugation by armed minorities or by outside pressures. . . . We must assist free peoples to work out their own destinies in their own way."

This is not to deny that the containment of Soviet power and influence—the organizing strategic principle of postwar U.S. foreign policy—was a necessity imposed by circumstances, but only to observe that the form and scope of containment were matters for debate and decision. Although events conspired to make it appear so, the militarization of containment was not preordained by the conditions prevailing in early postwar Europe. Certainly, after the Korean War, around the periphery of the Soviet empire from Southern Europe to rimland Asia, the extension of containment and the implicit commitment of U.S. military power were impelled by a powerful political and strategic logic—above all, by the desire to prevent further "miscalculations" of Western resolve and will. But, in principle at least, such a logic was compatible with a reserved right to discriminate among interests.

What accounted for both the specific form and broad reach of containment as they evolved in response to the events of the early Cold War was not merely the need to limit the expansion of Communist influence, but the conviction that to fail to respond to those events in the manner we did would be to put at risk the larger structure of international order that American power was committed to upholding and extending. It was the identification of containment with the principles on behalf of which we waged the Copld War, and our conviction that these were necessary to advance the broader purposes of American society, rather than the logic of containment, that led U.S. policymakers to conceive of the "imperatives" of strategy in the broad terms that they did. It was not the requirements of containment alone, but the conviction that the principles served by containment answered to a higher purpose—the cause of human freedom—that added to U.S. foreign policy the weight of moral necessity.

In the end, what made it possible to reconcile the traditional methods of statecraft with the revolutionary ends of U.S. policy was precisely the refusal to distinguish between the former and the latter. The promise that Cold War victory carried was not merely the "break-up or gradual mellowing of Soviet power" (to borrow George Kennan's famous phrase), but the vindication of essential principles of international order: "that acts of aggression and breaches of the peace ought to be suppressed, that disputes ought to be settled by peaceful means, that the basic human rights ought to be sustained, and that governments must cooperate across their frontiers in the great humanitarian purposes of mankind" (to cite Dean Rusk's formulation of a familiar American refrain).

The reconciliation between methods and purpose in U.S. policy, in short, was to be achieved prospectively. The order of the Cold War was not understood to be a direct reflection of the American purpose, but a necessary step toward the fulfillment of that purpose. The relationship between American values and the logic of world order was indirect, at best, and often remote. Indeed, the triumph of American values could hardly be achieved by force of arms; the purpose of American power was to provide an obstacle to aggression and a shield behind which the progress toward human freedom would be allowed to follow its natural course. It was this hope that linked the imperfect order of the Cold War to our expectations of a more just international society.

The clearest vindication of this expectation lies in the acceptance of the very principles in whose name we waged the Cold War by those who were, until very recently, our most determined adversaries. What is the "new thinking" of Soviet President Mikhail Gorbachev and his associates but the acceptance, in rhetoric at first, but now clearly also in substance, of the principles of international society that U.S. leaders have advocated since virtually the founding of our nation? Beyond this, however, the mostly pacific of revolutions of East-Central Europe, which has led to a renewal of national sovereignty and, in varying degrees, to a revival of democratic procedures, corroborates further the validity of the calculation underlying U.S. policy. Finally, both these developments have tended to complement the long-standing acceptance of the "new" principles of international order among the Western allies and our former enemies, Germany and Japan.

If the conclusion of the Cold War "on American terms" feels less like the end of an order and more like the beginning of an era in human history, one reason surely must be found in the unexampled concord that exists today among the world's great powers. Taken together, the industrialized countries of North America, Europe West and East (including Russia), and Japan account for a preponderant proportion of the world's output, control a similar share of the world's natural resources, cover as much as half of the world's territory and arable land, and virtually monopolize the production of new technologies, including nuclear weapons. Continued agreement among these nations cannot but have fundamental consequences for the future of human history.

VI

The triumph of Western, and preeminently American, principles of international organization in the Cold War heralds a new phase in the evolution of international politics. But how "new" will the new world be?

The truest measure of the impact of new thinking in international politics must be the extent to which it permits national leaders to transcend traditional patterns of thought and action. At its core, "new thinking" amounts to the reformulation, if not quite the rejection, of the traditional pattern and calculus of state policy. In the traditional view, as that view has been analyzed here, the vital interests of the state have been taken to represent a cardinal, virtually supreme value in the formulation and conduct of policy. In the past, absent the protective institutions of the state, the security of all other values must necessarily have been in doubt. It followed, therefore, that so long as the independence and survival of the state were the indispensable condition of all other values, these interests enjoyed, in practice if not in principle, an unrivaled primacy among political desiderata.

Have recent events altered this fundamental circumstance? Have the events of the past year in any way obviated the need to organize the collective force of the national community to preserve and protect the fundamental values of that community? In the first instance, it must be observed that whatever new order emerges from the one now ending will remain, at least for the foreseeable future, an order of states. Whatever qualifications national societies have accepted on their freedom of action, however enlightened the pursuit of national interests by today's political leaders, and however prompted by the imperatives of community with others, no great nation has yet abandoned its right to make these choices for itself or rejected the one institution capable of ensuring that right—the national state. This fact alone must set limits to the degree or quality and cast doubt on the permanence of international systemic change.

What is more, as the contributions to this volume make painfully evident, the principal inheritors of the old order each bring with them a remarkable continuity of historical interests. Thus, as John Van Oudenaren observes, the strategic aims of Gorbachev's vaunted program of "new thinking"—denuclearization of Europe and, more fundamentally, the tacit decoupling of U.S. and European defense forces—are barely distinguishable from those of Stalin, Khrushchev, and Brezhnev. These objectives correspond to the the most enduring historical interest of the Soviet-Russian state: to restructure the continental balance of power in its favor today by weakening Western Europe's Atlantic tie. The fact that Gorbachev has attempted to attain through self-denial what his predecessors sought to secure through threat and aggression may be attributed as much to the long-term weakening of the Soviet position as to the new Soviet leader's radical tactical flexibility.

As Anne Henderson points out, the Soviet turnaround in Eastern Europe was hardly motivated by generosity. The economies of Moscow's East European allies has long since ceased supporting the Soviet economy and had become a major drain on increasingly scarce Soviet resources. Seeking to unshoulder some of this burden, and seeing in Eastern Europe an enormous laboratory for the radical programs of restructuring that the new Soviet leadership hoped to implement at home, Moscow began to distance itself from its erstwhile clients. When it became clear that a massive use of force would be needed to preserve the Eastern empire after Communist governments began to weaken and fall throughout the region, the Soviets were restrained from upholding their allies for fear that to do so would be to destroy hard-earned gains in Western Europe. Forced to weigh the political space and potential financial support gained in the West for *perestroika*, a policy that had itself become identified with the revitalization and long-term survival of the Russian state, the Soviet leadership determined that the price of the Brezhnev Doctrine had become too high.

On the other hand, the consequences that have followed from Gorbachev's radical departures underscores not only the desperation of the current Soviet leadership, but also the dangers that must accrue from any policy that fails to attend to the necessity of preserving the vitality and coherence of the state. By abandoning its position in Eastern Europe, including Germany, the Soviet leadership gave up not only its most important source of geopolitical leverage against the West, but invited a similar chain of events within the borders of the Soviet state. If the ultimate consequence of adherence to the principles of "new thinking" should turn out to be the rapid breakup of Soviet power and the strategic isolation of the Russian Republic, it may not be only the old system of Communist domination that will have been discredited, but also the "new thinking" that allegedly induced these developments.

Should such developments transpire, a weak, truncated Russia stranded at the heart of the Eurasian landmass and surrounded by enemies may prove far more dangerous to international order than the Communist empire ever was.

Continuity of state interest is evident in German policy as well. The end of the Cold War dispensation—the division not only of Europe but of the German nation—returns to the top of continental politics an agenda that for more than a century has rocked, and twice nearly destroyed, Europe: how to balance the legitimate claims and dynamic energy of a great state at the center of Europe against the equally legitimate claims of general European security and order.

The central problem of that history, as Josef Joffe points out, was not so much resolved as suppressed by Germany's postwar division. The two Germanys' acceptances of fundamental qualifications on their sovereignty and indeed their very nationhood shortly after World War II reflected not an abandonment of the traditional purposes of German diplomacy—what Joffe calls "the quest for reduced dependence and increased options"—but a pragmatic accommodation to circumstance. Forced to choose between a radically circumscribed independence and uncertain future in the Western and Eastern alliances and the risks of isolation and permanent division that attended a more assertive policy aimed at national reconstitution, the leaders of both Germanys in the early Cold War accepted the tangible, if bittersweet rewards of community with the victors. In the West, Konrad Adenauer's choice was made easier by the economic benefits of participation in the open West European economic zone. By the same token, the limited foothold on sovereignty that he gained later provided an adequate platform from which politicians of a different ideological stripe were able to pursue a distinctively German agenda in the East even under the relative confinement of West Germany's radical dependence on the West.

No longer held hostage by its division, a reunited German nation is now freed of its most burdensome constraint. The new Germany, for reasons of its own, may not choose to abandon its slowly crafted and carefully nurtured relations with the West in favor of a neutralist, or even more openly nationalistic, posture in the middle of Europe. The point is that the principle conditions that have prevented it from doing so in the past have now vanished.

If Germany remains "anchored" in the West after reunification, it will be because and for as long as the Germans desire to be so anchored. Participation in the Atlantic Alliance is no longer the condition of German sovereignty. NATO's deterrent umbrella is not one that all Germans appreciate or that German industry is incapable of supplying. And for this reason, NATO's levers are singularly inappropriate as constraints on German autonomy: to apply them with any force—in the extreme, to expel Germany from the Western defense community—is to force upon the Germans the very choices we wish them to avoid.

The fact that the only plausible German "threat" today is that of economic, rather than military, dominance poses a new kind of strategic dilemma. On the one hand, the attempt to constrain German economic might through military (that is, alliance) pressures is at best inappropriate and, if it fuels German resentment or isolation, dangerous. On the other hand, Germany's economic access to the West (or East) is no longer, and probably never has been, something that can be profitably (or practically) denied by the allied powers.

The dissolution of the most palpable structural restraints on German policy—including, it should be observed, the proximity of Soviet power—has increased the salience of more traditional state interests in both Western and East-Central Europe. Like Germany, but under quite different circumstances and constraints, French policy, too, has consistently aimed at regaining control over the national destiny. The idea of "Europe," as Simon Serfaty shows, gained momentum as French leaders perceived in it a compensation for France's own inherent weaknesses and a protection against the different strengths and presumptions of (West) Germany and the two superpowers. And it stalled when the French president became suspicious of the nation (Britain) upon which he had hoped to rely both as a necessary counterweight to German influence and as throw-weight for a "Europe" independent of American tutelage.

Unfortunately, for France's national aspirations, as for Britain's even more recently, the imperatives of community as the vehicle of lasting national recovery have proven inescapable. Worse, the dilemma of European unity—how to build a "Europe" that includes Germany, as it must, without being effectively absorbed by that nation, as it might—has only been sharpened over time. First, the relative economic balance between France and Germany has deteriorated noticeably, and France's dependency has increased even more pointedly during recent decades. Second, the end of the Cold War has invalidated a key implicit, if not altogether unnoticed, assumption of all postwar schemes for integration: the permanence of German division. The removal of Germany's last material fetters has revealed, as no other event could, both the compelling necessity and inescapable risks of France's collective strategy for national renewal.

In East-Central Europe, finally, the former associates of the Warsaw Treaty Organization face, in far less favorable circumstances, an economic dilemma similar to that of Western Europe—and a political dilemma that may prove even less tractable. Economically, the former Eastern bloc states have little more than their own acute needs to guide policy; to balance the attractiveness of German capital, little more than their ardent desire for support from other sources. In the short run, the danger of a loss of control over their national destiny resulting from their extreme economic dependency must seem barely palpable, if not altogether spurious, in light of the more immediate dangers of outright financial collapse or social disintegration.

Politically, as George Liska argues, the present condition of East-Central Europe carries a far greater danger for the evolution of global politics. A heady East-Central European nationalism that is either agressively anti-Russian or modestly neutral risks either accelerating the breakup of the Soviet empire by providing an example and a goad to independence for the Soviet Union's westernmost republics or, to the extent that the old national and ethnic conflicts that kept Eastern Europe weak and divided revive, creating a vacuum of power that, following historical precedent, is most likely to result in either Russo-German antagonism or condominium in the heart of Europe and at the center of the global power structure.

The first possibility is most likely to result not from the ambitions of either of the two great powers, but from a cycle of reaction and counter-reaction arising from a Soviet attempt to avoid strategic isolation and a German desire to preserve access to Europe's eastern hinterland. The second possibility is but a pragmatic and time-honored method of containing the explosive tendencies of the first. The only remedy to these dangers, moreover, is a kind of self-restraint involving acceptance of limitations on the prerogatives of national sovereignty that few states, and none that have newly regained their independence, have proven willing to accept.

VII

In sum, the end of the Cold War has hardly banished the ancient agenda of European politics from history. To the contrary, the collapse of the Cold War dispensation has returned the claims of state interest to the stage of European and world politics almost, one might say, with a vengeance. Does it inevitably follow, then, that what must result is a return to the traditional calculus and methods of international politics? Is the promise of "new thinking" nothing more than a chimera or, at best, a momentary and fleeting glimpse of the possibilities of a future that lies far beyond present circumstances? Must the future hold nothing more than the disappointment of all the profound hopes that inspired and justified the sacrifices of the past 40 years?

If the promise of "new thinking" depended entirely upon the abandonment of the claims of state interest, the answer to all of these questions would necessarily be affirmative. But the promise of "new thinking" does not require that the traditional claims of state interest be exorcised from history—only that the pursuit of those claims become more enlightened. The point to be noticed in contemporary international politics is not only the reemergence of tradional fears and interests, but the consistent willingness of great states to pursue them by means that are cooperative rather than competitive and of leaders to pay heed to the imperatives of community that are broader than merely national.

Thus, if it is true that the motives behind Soviet advocacy of "new thinking" both at home and abroad are motivated by enduring national concerns, it is also true that the methods employed stand the traditional calculus of reason of state on its head. From a broad view, the recent departures of Soviet policy continue to respond to the imperatives of national interest, aimed as they are at dissolving the Western coalition against Soviet power and gaining equal, if not preferential, access to the whole of Europe, the dissolution of Soviet Russia's Eastern empire, and the approach taken so far to the national question within the confines of the Soviet Union must also be taken as evidence of the degree to which traditional definitions of Soviet interest have been sacrificed to the imperatives of community with the West. The risks now confronting Soviet leaders may have been difficult to avoid over the long term, and perhaps even the short run, but because they have been accepted so freely provides a clear indicator of the quality of change in the patterns of Soviet thought.

A similar refinement of understanding evidently informs German policy today. If the most immediate and compelling external restraints on German policy have been removed, the need for self-restraint has not. Having achieved unity, Germany is not freed of the need to propitiate its former adversaries and allies: the Soviet Union through economic support; France and "Europe" through acceptance of deeper integration; the United States and Europe through voluntary acceptance of the "binding" ties of NATO (that is, through a continued willingness to accept the implicit constraints of strategic dependency under the American nuclear umbrella and the firm rejection of neutralism—a formula for unilateralism that is unworkable without nuclear weapons and even more dangerous with them).

German policy may be only conditionally conservative; it is perhaps impossible to know for certain. In the short-run, the immediate objective, whatever the long-range design, must be to consolidate the advantageous position suddenly (but not quite unpredictably) conferred on the German nation by the events of 1989. In time, however, given the range of options made available to German leaders by the new European dispensation, the choice of a different policy must remain open to a degree that the circumstances of few other states allow.

By the same token, however, the implicit constraints to which current German policy responds—the dangers of strategic isolation and a repetition of previous cycles of European and world history—are unlikely to be weakened in time (even though they may begin to chafe), while the positive inducements of community are more likely to be increased by accommodation to the imperatives of integration than through a narrowly conceived attempt to exploit national advantage. Moreover, the restrictions on German freedom of action should be made more bearable to the extent that they are accepted as a matter of choice and no longer embedded in a structure that mutilates the body politic and denies to German ingenuity and dynamism equal access to the world.

France, too, finds itself compelled by considerations of national interest to accept qualifications on its sovereignty that in another age, or indeed no more than two decades ago, would have been scarcely imaginable. The reemergence of a strong and united Germany strengthens, the imperative of community for France precisely because now more than ever "Europe" provides the formula most conducive to a revival of French national strength while providing the most effective means of diluting German political and economic power. As risks have increased, options have narrowed, but the French response, no less than the Russian and German, stands the traditional calculus of reason of state on its head. Just as de Gaulle once insisted that there could be no "Europe" without France, so the present French leadership has come to the conclusion that there can be no France outside of "Europe."

The paradox of French national strategy—the attempt to retain maximum control over national destiny through the sacrifice of unfettered state sovereignty—may be made to stand for a more pervasive dilemma confronting each of the great powers of the modern international system. If the order that has succeeded the postwar order remains an order of states, it is also an order in which the fate of the great states has become so closely intertwined that none dares stand alone, and all demonstrate a circumspect regard for the vital interests of another. The order that has emerged is typified in its substance by an ineluctable chain of overlapping mutual dependencies and compensations. What has changed in the world now emerging from the dark age of the Cold War are neither the needs or ambitions of nations, but the circumstances in which these must be pursued. For all powers, now the great no less than the small, the imperatives of community act as a restraint on the imperatives of national survival, not because the former are expedient to the latter, but because they have become indispensable.

VIII

For more than four centuries, conflicts in and about Europe invariably have become the world's conflicts. And during the past four decades, in a sense that is perilously literal, the fate of the world hung on the ability of two superpowers to avoid war over Europe. The reason in both cases is simple: The Continent has long contained the largest concentration of military and industrial might on the planet. In geopolitical terms, the promise of "new thinking" is one in which the threat of global war will have been dissipated, if not altogether expunged, by the establishment of an order—a "common

European home"—in which Europe is finally at peace with itself.

It is unfortunate that in a world of states, even one so radically transformed from past orders as the one in which we now live, there can be no guarantee that the imperatives of community will always coexist with and constrain the imperatives of national survival. The order of "new thinking," because it will remain an order of states, may therefore differ from past orders in quality, but not in kind. The promise of the new order cannot be to dispense with the need to continue to organize the collective power of national communities nor, hence, to dispense with that requisite of order among states—the balance of power. Moreover, the servitudes of power will continue to set limits to the scope and quality of the community that can be conceived. The order of new thinking will be constructed and extended, if it can be constructed at all, first among the strong, and then in Europe only. Within Europe, in other words, the new order will remain an order of power, even if it approaches justice more closely than any order of the past. Outside of Europe, the world may be little better off—indeed, as Ilya Prizel suggests, it may be worse off.

It will also be, finally, an order that relies crucially upon American power as the reserve to supply for the deficits of community and interest. The events of the past 40 years have not left us unaffected. We have payed a price at home and abroad for the role we undertook to play in the world. Yet, the record of the past and the promise of the future should provide sufficient incentive to encourage rededication and recommitment to the purposes that have brought us this far.

Index